# Adva

In her new book *“Different: what your special needs kid wants you to know,”* Sally Ross Brown has reached into her personal experience growing up as a special needs kid, her knowledge of both disability and parenting and into her heart to create a bright light of love and wisdom. Filled with wise advice, laughter and joy, Brown's succinct words and verbal gems are a pure gift to frightened parents facing the heart wrenching opportunity of raising a special needs child, and an affirmation for all of us who have ever loved a child.

– Nancy Edwards, PhD, Psychologist Emeritus in Minnesota, Retired Special Education Teacher and Administrator

In an honest and insightful voice, Sally Brown invites us to grow through her lived experience. In “*Different*”, we are all invited to learn how diversity and acceptance create the beauty we are.

– Ali Sands author of “*I Know Who You Are, but What am I?*”

If you have a family member with special needs, you need this special book. It's written by an amazing woman who tells you what she wishes her mom had known. This one is Different. It's a keeper. If I had known growing up that my family and I weren't alone, it might have changed everything. This book would have been under my pillow.

– Doris A Taylor, Ph.D., FACC, FAHA

"Everything I ever needed to hear, but didn't, from someone I trusted that has lived the experience."

-Jenn Alex Brockman

Special Needs Mom

# Different

## WHAT YOUR SPECIAL NEEDS CHILD WANTS YOU TO KNOW

By Sally Ross Brown

Wilmington, DE

Copyright © 2020 Sally Ross Brown. All rights reserved. No portion of this book may be reproduced mechanically, electronically, or by any other means, including photocopying, without written permission from the author. It is illegal to copy this book, post it to a website, or distribute it by any other means without permission from the author.

SallyRossBrown.com

Thomas Noble Books
Wilmington, DE
www.thomasnoblebooks.com
ISBN: 978-1-945586-26-2
First Printing: 2020
Editing by Gwen Hoffnagle

This publication is designed to provide accurate and authoritative information regarding the subject matter covered. It is sold with the understanding that the author is not engaged in rendering professional services. If legal, accounting, medical, psychological, or any other expert assistance is required, the services of a competent professional person should be sought.

# DEDICATION

**For Vickie**

Who never gave up on this book and who loves me enough to make me brave enough to write it.

# Table of Contents

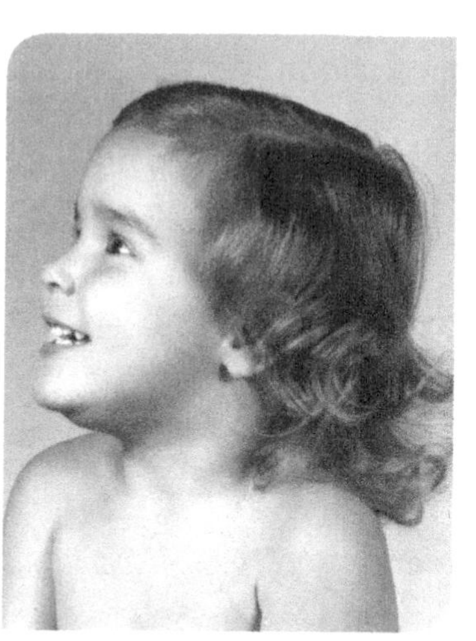

# Introduction

I'm a grown woman living with cerebral palsy. Much of my life has been and continues to be rich and wonderful. It seems to me the longer I live, the better it gets. It's also true that I never remember not feeling different. I never remember not feeling "less than perfect."

When I was a child my disability was often front and center in my mind. I measured experiences by how I was able to perform. Could I do what everybody else did? And if I couldn't, I needed to react so that nobody really knew how disappointed I was. It was my biggest secret.

I learned early that if I seemed totally comfortable with my differences, the people around me were more comfortable too. I also learned that if I seemed totally okay, people thought I was brave or wonderful or some such thing. I remember being puzzled about this reaction, but I was very certain that I needed to maintain my accepting attitude no matter what.

The only person who knew what I worked so hard to hide was my "Steel Magnolia" of a mother. She was a Southern belle of the highest order. In those early years I never remember her leaving the house without a full face of makeup and a girdle on her already slender body. She was a force. She knew how things were supposed to be and I don't think it ever occurred to her that they would not be exactly as she had planned. In fact, I was born simply because she would not give up.

After my older brother's birth she had a stillborn child; and before I was born she had another baby who lived only a few days. The story goes that my dad and the doctors all begged her not to try again. I'm not sure why they bothered. Sixty-seven years later I'm here to tell you that not having me was simply out of the question. I was a preemie, around thirty weeks, born in 1952, weighing a little over two pounds. I have no doubt that my mother simply willed me to survive.

When I was about two my parents began to notice that I was missing milestones and realized something might be wrong. One of my favorite family stories is that doctors tried to explain to my mother that I might never walk. Her only response was, "Well of course she will walk."

There were some amazing benefits to having such a powerhouse of a mother. One of the best things she did was create experiences that leveled the playing field for me, long before anybody had ever even imagined the Americans with Disabilities Act (ADA) or disability rights.

One year our Brownie troop was supposed to march in the Christmas parade. She called the chamber of commerce to inform them that our troop was not going to march but would be riding in the back of a pickup truck. The Chevrolet dealership lent us a brand new truck, which she decorated as Candyland, and to this day I still remember how much fun we had. All the other troops were jealous and the girls in Troop 185 were more than a little bit full of ourselves.

She was also that mom who took us to the most fun places. Every year my parents loaded up the station wagon and took a carload of us to Memphis to Holiday on Ice. We spent the night in the Admiral Benbow Inn and had breakfast at IHOP, which was a delicacy for us, even though Clarksdale, Mississippi, then had, and still has, some of the greatest Southern cuisine on the planet. Looking back, I now realize it was the social event of the year for me and my friends.

I have lots of wonderful memories, like that, experiences my mother made happen that I still reminisce about with my oldest friends, and we're almost seventy. I always loved that my mom was so good to my friends. They were always welcome in our home, and I was proud to be that girl with a cool mom who everyone wanted to be around.

However, one day I heard my mother talking to one of her friends. They were discussing all the things my parents did with all the kids and my mom said, "I always thought maybe Sally needed a little help." As I write this, I can still feel that punch in the gut that I felt all those years ago. Everything she did for us and the places she took us were so much fun, but had she really thought that nobody would like me if she didn't do it?

Yet to my adult self, who has loved and been a part of raising kids and grandkids, it now seems like a really sweet thing to have said. It's something I can see myself saying about the kids I love today. My mother knew that my seven-year-old heart broke a little every single time I sat out because I couldn't quite keep up. And she knew that I was determined to never let anybody see how I felt.

She was my safe place, my rock. Countless times I would come in from outside and break into tears because I had missed out on something, telling her how embarrassed I felt about being unable to do it because of my disability. Sometimes she was gentle and understanding, even rubbing my legs, which often hurt because my muscles where so tight. Some days, though, she would be angry with me and say things like "Sally, feeling sorry for yourself is very unattractive" or "Misery is always optional." It always felt like a crap shoot as to which mom I would get on any given day.

Now I'm extremely grateful for both moms. Was her timing always perfect, and did I always get exactly what I needed at the exact right time? I don't think so. That is certainly not how I remember it. She had all the same feelings about cerebral palsy (CP) that I did. She was sad some days and disappointed that I was not more typical, and just knowing this made me furious. Some days I was convinced she was totally embarrassed and wished she had a different kid. One day I was so angry with her that I shaved off one of my eyebrows just because I knew she would hate that. This type of battle raged throughout my grade school years. We lived this life together, doing this dance in secret from the outside world.

I think there *were* probably a lot of days when she wished she had a different kid. It might or might not have had much to do with my disability, but regardless of what others may have thought, we were not living in a Hallmark movie. There were no easy answers, even fewer easy days, and we forged on.

But there were gifts that came from living with a disability too. I know it has made me more patient, and kinder. I know how hard it can be to be different. I know firsthand that people are not always as confident as they seem, and I've learned that the magic of loving comes when you're lucky enough to have people show you their most authentic selves. I believe that my CP helped me learn to create safe spaces for people to share with me on a deep level, whether in a single moment or over the course of a lifetime. It has been the greatest gift of my life, and I learned that from my mother.

If you're raising a child with special needs, I wrote this book for you. You're navigating a journey you could never have imagined for yourself. You might also realize that you're not special, or strong, or particularly brave, and you're not interested in inspiring anyone; you just wanted a healthy, typical kid.

I am by no means an expert. I am not a doctor. What I have to share is what I've learned growing up with cerebral palsy. The effects of my CP are mild, and I consider myself to be very lucky. I know that many of your children have bigger challenges than mine. Even so, I'm hoping that some of what is written here rings true with you. I want to help you get a glimpse of how perfect you are, even in the darkest times – even when you have no idea what to do next.

I started creating this book years ago as part of my grief journey after my mother died. It seemed like she was always on my mind and my emotions were all over the map. Some days I was angry; some days I was so sad I could hardly breathe. I wanted an accurate picture of who she was and a clear understanding of what our relationship had been. I journaled feverishly about it. I dreamed about her. There was a piece of her I needed to define, to explain to myself. There seemed to be so many things I had needed to say and hadn't. It felt like we had unfinished business. I wanted her to know that I was fine and that she had done a good job. Eventually, after many tough days, weeks, and months, I wrote this to her:

## A Note to Special Parents (from a special kid)

**1. You are the perfect parents for me.**

I know you didn't sign up for a kid like me. I also know you sometimes think you can't face what it takes to raise me. I want you to know that this isn't true. I believe I chose you. Whatever you need to learn, you will learn. The strength you think you need will come from somewhere. The people you need to meet will show up when you need them.

**2. This is the perfect life for me.**

My life is a very special one. I believe I will impact the world in a unique and wonderful way. Remember this when your heart is breaking because you want a path for me that is so much easier than this one.

**3. I need you to find your own spiritual paths.**

The road we're on is not an easy one. To be successful, you'll need all the spiritual strength you can muster for the tough days. You'll need to help me when my spiritual strength is out the window. You'll often see signs of my determination and be amazed by it. That's not enough. You'll have to find your own answers. I'm depending on you for that.

**4. However you feel about me is okay.**

Sometimes you'll feel tired and helpless, and it will seem like you won't be able to provide care for me for one more day. Sometimes you'll be angry because there seems to be no escaping me. That's okay. There's no way you can take care of me without having those days.

Sometimes you might watch people look at me and be a bit embarrassed that I'm not doing better. That doesn't make you a bad parent; it just means you're human.

When you face many of these days in a row, it's time for you to get somebody else to take care of me, just long enough for you to regenerate yourself. It's always important to let people help you. I'm depending on you to do whatever you need to do to take care of yourself.

**5. However I feel about my disability is okay.**

Some days you'll be amazed at how content I am, and you'll wonder how in the world I do it. Treasure those days. Some days I'll be discouraged; some days I'll be angry; and some days I'll even feel really sorry for myself. Don't panic. I'll come back around again. If you let me express these unattractive feelings, they have much less power. Even typical folks feel sorry for themselves sometimes.

**6. Let me try things I want to try even if you're sure I'll fail.**

I know you want to protect me – that's your job; I'm your child. But I need you to understand that my survival depends on my determination. Part of my process is to figure out what my limitations really are. Sometimes I will want to try to do things that seem impossible to you. Please encourage me anyway. It's the willingness to try that's important – success is a bonus. If I fail, I'll get over it.

**7. Don't worry about my whole life today.**

You'll worry about how my life will turn out. You'll lose hours of sleep trying to figure out how I'll survive in the world after you're gone. This isn't helpful to me. Just help me focus on today. The more you can focus on whatever we have to face today, the more you'll be helping me develop the skills I'll need when it's time for me to get along without you.

**8. Sometimes people will be mean to me or scared of me. I expect you to stick up for me, but I don't expect you to change the world.**

There are a lot of really wonderful people in the world. You and I will meet many of them. But there will also be those who are afraid of me or don't treat me fairly. They'll assume things about me that aren't true. They may even assume things about you that aren't true. I expect you to speak up for me when you can, but I also need you to be able to let it go. It won't help me if you're angry and defensive all the time. If you are, there might be those who won't want to help me just because it's too hard for them to deal with you.

**9. Finding good doctors and professionals is important, but you know me better than they do. I expect you to trust your own instincts about what's good for me.**

The doctors and therapists who work with me are very important for the quality of my life. Some of them will be amazing and others won't be. It will often be up to you to decide which is which. Listen to them and know that what they say is important, but also remember that you know me best. If something they suggest doesn't feel right to you, listen to that small voice in your head and speak up.

**10. I really hope we can laugh.**

I believe laughing was probably God's best idea. It's the one thing that can bring joy to our lives the quickest. If I get stuck in a mud puddle, it's probably funny. If you're lifting me and we both fall on the floor in a heap, that's probably funny too. A good joke is worth taking the time to laugh at. Help me not get so caught up in the serious problems we face every day to forget about laughing.

* * *

I'm not sure where those words came from. At the time they felt more dictated to me than something I created. I was sorry I had not been able to share these thoughts with my mother, but I committed then and there that I would share them with other special parents.

There's a chance you've seen these "10 Things" before. They're on lots of websites, and some hospitals include them in information they give to new parents when special kids are born. Over the years I've communicated with many parents who found the 10 Things helpful. It has been and continues to be my greatest privilege to get to know these parents and to let them (and now you!) know who I am.

This book is intended to be an expansion of the 10 Things. It's a series of short sayings to give you a little boost of love whenever you need it. I tried to write the entries so they can be read in no more than thirty seconds. I figure that on most days that's about all the extra time you have!

I promise that whatever you bring to this life every single day is exactly enough. You're exactly what your child needs, just as you are. You are what they need on the great days, the over-the-top joyful days, and those days when you're hanging by a thread.

The sayings are divided into chapters. Each chapter starts with a short essay that gives you some thoughts from my point of view as an adult who grew up learning to manage life with a disability.

Keep this book where you can grab it when you need it. Mark it up. Dog-ear the pages that ring true. My wish is that some of the things written here touch your heart and help you understand that you are amazing, that your child is amazing, and that you can always trust yourself to do the next right thing.

For a free printable poster of The 10 Things, visit SallyRossBrown.com

# CHAPTER 1

# For New Parents of Special Needs Children

You'll notice in this chapter (and throughout this book) that I write a lot about how hard things are and will become. I write about insecurity and fear. I write about exhaustion and isolation. These feelings are part of your parenting journey. You will always be making decisions about how to deal with them. Some days you'll do far better than on other days, and some days you'll be asking yourself how you can possibly go more one day. There's only one reason to keep going, and that's the unconditional love you feel toward your special child. It's unescapable.

When your child was born, maybe you felt this love right away, and maybe it took some time. Every path is different. But you can count on this love. You won't feel it every moment of every day, but it's there. Every day I'm still blown away by the power of the love that grows in special needs families. Yours is no different. And if you haven't felt it yet, don't worry. You will.

In the following passages, I cover some of the challenges you will face and the uncertainties that will inevitably haunt you in the early days, and I attempt to provide courage and understanding so that you know you're not alone in this difficult but oh-so-rewarding journey.

## Life Long Parenting

Now that you're raising a special kiddo, your feelings about disability will inevitably change. Before you had a special child, watching other parents with special kids in public felt very different from the way it feels now. You might have made some assumptions about what their lives must be like and what's possible for the child with the disability.

All of those previously held ideas are still there – and even if you don't realize it, on a gut level you still believe a lot of those things. It can make you feel terribly guilty and it might even gnaw at you.

Be easy on yourself about your old beliefs. But remember those old beliefs even as you shed them. They help you understand the people around you and how to teach them about your child.

## When families receive a special needs diagnosis for their child it becomes a major family focus

Somewhere in almost every home with a special needs child is a notebook or a drawer or stacks and stacks of paper that contain reports, test results, and evaluations from endless doctors and therapists. This information is important because the more you know the more you can help your kiddo be the best they can be.

But those documents can also be incredibly scary. It's so easy to read about your child's strengths and weaknesses written in black and white. It may cause you to consider the future with a real sense of dread. Remember this: *your child is not their diagnosis*; it's just a small part of who they are. Your child is the wonderful, magical little person you watch every day, and is unique and special in their own right, just like every child. Embrace that, trust that. The diagnosis is a roadmap – a guide to help direct you toward information that might help. It's not the final word on who your child will be.

## One of the hardest things about having a child with special needs is that there is a better-than-average chance that some parenting responsibilities will last for the rest of your life

It might be obvious even now that growing up and moving on in the usual way is not going to happen with your kid. That can be too overwhelming to take in all at once, so please don't take on the worries of forever today. It takes the joy and peace out of today and you still must live through it in the future.

When fear and dread of the future seep into your mind and heart, consciously set them aside. Some days you might have to do this every five minutes. With purposeful practice, leaving the future *in the future* gets easier. Dwelling on uncertainties is not worth giving up the gifts of today.

## What did I do wrong?

You thought you could "earn" safety and success for your family if you did right by the world and prayed often. You did that, and you still had a child who has special needs. How did this happen to you? To your family?

These kinds of questions are part of the process you need to go through to find peace with this life you hadn't planned for. Some version of this questioning, and even feeling betrayed by God, is part of this journey for every parent. There's never going to be an easy answer. Your understanding and beliefs about this will be forever changing.

Some days you'll feel like you have no faith in anything. You'll feel like you hate the Universe. Like everything you ever believed was a lie. You think you will be spiritually empty forever. There's nothing you can do about those days and those feelings. Give yourself permission to have them. You will not have to "pay" or be punished for feeling those feelings. If you can accept them as part of you, you will be able to move past them into a peace.

It will come. Today just put one foot in front of the other and do the next right thing.

## Doctors, Therapists, Teachers and Social Workers

The ebb and flow of your days often revolve around such professionals. Making appointments, driving, waiting, driving more, waiting longer, and hoping for callbacks are draining and can be infuriating. But remember that some of these professionals will work miracles. If it weren't for certain physicians, your child might not even be here.

You know your child the absolute best. You see the subtle changes when you try new medication and when diets and routines are altered. The dance you do with the professionals is not easy. You're charged with balancing what you know about your child against the knowledge and expertise of those who have been trained to treat your child's specific issues. Please be willing to keep an open mind when recommendations are made, yet speak up when your intuition says they're the wrong path for your child.

Sometimes you may look back and regret something you decided to do or not do. Regrets are wasted energy. If a different option seems better in hindsight, please let it go. Trust that you made the best decision you could have in the moment.

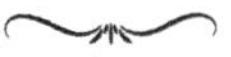

## There are dreams you once had for your child that are not going to happen

At least they're not going to happen in the way you first pictured them. Letting go of your original beliefs about raising your child is a lifelong process. There will be days when you decide to accept what is true and find joy in it. You can see your child as a child first, and the more you bond with them the less the differences matter. They're funny, they love life and the people around them, and maybe they don't have a single mean bone in their body.

But even in the middle of love, acceptance, and the moments you will cherish forever, the old dreams of "normal" come back and you become sad. Then you feel guilty.

How can you expect the world to accept your child just the way they are if you can't? Let your feelings be what they are. Even on a good day you may feel that familiar ache of what you had wanted for them. It's part of you; it's part of this journey. You are exactly where you should be today.

## In the Early Days of Discovering That Your Child Has Special Needs, You Might Feel Like You Will Never Laugh Again

It feels like moments of lightheartedness and laughter are gone forever. The world seems sad and heavy and it feels like it will be that way forever.

Like so much of what you'll think early on, that's not at all how it will turn out. You'll become more grateful for the smallest things, and if you're willing to pay attention, you can find so much wonder in the day-to-day of this unexpected life. By necessity, you'll move more slowly. You'll see things you never noticed before. A good day, or a good nap, can feel like a great gift. One mealtime that goes off without a hitch can be a welcome surprise.

I want you to notice the small and wonderful things in an ordinary day. If a few days go by and you realize you're not smiling or laughing, pay closer attention. Those wonderful moments are always there. Stay committed to acknowledging them.

## Every now and then you'll have "dumpster days"

Those are days when everything you touch seems to fall to pieces. On those days all you can do is just make sure everybody is still alive. You have no spiritual connection to anything. You can hardly even look at your kid. Everything is too much. You're too tired to be anything but numb. You think maybe you should reach out to let somebody know how badly you feel, but it's too much of an effort to even do that. All you seem to be able to do is sit and stare.

These days happen. Even if you do everything right, they happen. They also happen in families with typically developing kids. They just do.

Learn to accept them as part of the process. Pay attention to them. If dumpster days happen more than occasionally, you need more help. Be committed to reaching out when you need to, especially when it's the last thing you want to do.

## Almost nothing about this journey goes in a straight line

Even long periods of unbelievable progress can be interrupted by an unexpected setback. Treatments and medications that were miraculous in the beginning begin to be less effective. A new symptom pops up. An old, almost forgotten symptom returns. Any of these things can be devastating. That's just how this works. It's kind of how life works too. Sometimes we need to have old ideas quit working so we can get to the next better idea. Progress is always a moving target.

Learn to celebrate day-to-day progress. The setbacks are never easy, but know that they happen. A year from now, or six months from now, today's crisis will be a distant memory.

If you look at all the progress you've made so far, you might fondly remember it as a nice, smooth arc always moving upward. In reality, it's been a series of stops and starts.

Setbacks do not have to rob you of hope. They can be the fastest way to get to the next promising idea.

## Savor the precious moments

Many days with your child will be magical. There will be indescribable moments when you see past the disability and struggle straight into the heart of your beautiful child. Months of work in therapy will pay off and a long-coveted milestone will be conquered. There will be times they meet your eyes with theirs and you both feel that connection that only you two have.

At those moments you are more joyful than you thought you could ever be. Hold on to those – savor them. This is where you get your strength for the days when all you can do is put one foot in front of the other and keep moving. Trust that the joyful days will carry you through the difficult ones.

## Kids will ask questions

"Why does he have a wheelchair?" "Can he walk?" "Why doesn't he talk?" Stuff like that. In these situations the kids are the easy part, and the hard part is that their parents are usually mortified. Before your child came along you might have been uncomfortable with disabilities too. Maybe you thought the polite thing to do was not notice.

Take the time to answer questions. Help make it okay to ask. The the more people there are who know about your child, the easier it will be for your child to navigate the world. Even if you're tired, which may seem like always, try to take the time to engage with people who are curious. The more it's okay for others to ask about the differences, the easier it is for them to see the similarities between special needs children and the rest of the world.

## It's hard to be patient

You feel like you need to push forward. You have a special kid to fight for! You do a little more research, find one more therapist, add something new to your home therapy program. There must be something else you can do to help your child move forward faster, right? There must be!

It's easy to think that your worth as a parent depends on how hard you push every day. You want to help your child learn that they do have some control over their disability if they're willing to put in the work. Working hard *is* important, but it's okay to let your child help you set the pace.

Sometimes you'll struggle to meet milestones and both of you will become frustrated. But then, in your child's own time – when it's the right time – you'll find that they've found their own way. Please be patient with yourself as you try to find the balance between pushing for progress and allowing your child to do things their own way, in their own time. Patience is a virtue for a reason; and never more important than now.

## Reaching or missing a milestone is something you'll think about incessantly

"Will he walk?" "Will he speak?" "When?" "What if he doesn't?" As soon as his first word comes out, it's easy to skip to "Will he put sentences together?"

But simply sitting up unassisted for thirty seconds could very well be a major breakthrough. Don't miss celebrating these milestones. Give each step forward its' moment. Your child deserves it. You all deserve it. Every single success comes from work. *Lots* of it. Trips to the therapist. Therapy at home. Living through tantrums.

You will all keep moving forward. You will do the next thing that makes sense. No matter how diligent or determined you all are, the changes will always come in their own time. The "when" of it is none of your business.

You deserve to enjoy the success and progress of hard work.

## EVERY MEMBER OF YOUR FAMILY HAS FEELINGS ABOUT YOUR CHILD WITH SPECIAL NEEDS AND HOW THOSE NEEDS AFFECT THE FAMILY

Your special kiddo will find their way, but their siblings and your spouse are also figuring out how they fit in this family. It's different for each of you on any given day. The journey is not an easy one. There are just some days and times that are hard – it's. You cannot make it fair. Life is not fair.

But what you can do is talk about what you know about your special needs child. If you have the doctor's firm diagnosis and the information that comes with it, share it with everyone in the family unit. A diagnosis is a roadmap, and if it feels like a secret it will have the power to separate you. Don't feel ashamed to say the diagnosis out loud.

The disability in your family is only a part of who you are together. Being open and easy about discussing it is a big part of experiencing the special joy that comes with this special life you're living. Talk, be honest, and don't hide your feelings about the disability from each other. Your special child will strengthen your family unit in many wonderful ways.

## Children who have siblings with special needs have a challenging journey

It's never going to be fair or even for all your children. Trying to make it so is deadly for parents. Be very gentle with yourself and with your typical kiddos. They get to be angry sometimes, and they get to express their frustration. Set aside time for each of your children as best you can. Try to make sure there are time and resources for them to do some of the things they're interested in. Sometimes it works. Sometimes it doesn't.

Your typical children will develop some priceless gifts from being raised in your family. It's more likely than not that they will be blessed with great empathy and acceptance of others that will enrich their lives always. Just don't expect to see it in them every day. Allow them to navigate this life their own way. Their path to peace and acceptance isn't a straight line either.

## There's no feeling you can feel that means you don't love your child

When you're raising a special needs child, a lot of the feelings you feel about your child don't match what you expected to be feeling. There were the dreams you had before they were born – those dreams are gone or at least drastically changed from your original fantasies, yet they're still imprinted on your heart. For as long as you live there will be a little part of you that's still sad about the loss of those dreams.

The work you do to take care of your child can be physically, mentally, and emotionally exhausting. As a payoff for your challenging work there is often progress, but sometimes that's not the case. When progress does come it's most often in tiny steps. You will be frustrated. You will be angry. And some days you will feel totally overwhelmed. You will ask yourself more than once, "Why am I not taking my kid to soccer practice instead of therapy?"

None of this makes you a bad parent. None of this means you're not doing what's best for your child.

None of this means you're not a tireless champion for your amazing child. You are. Be gentle with yourself.

## You will not win every battle

One of the infuriating things about the life of a special needs parent is how ridiculously hard you must fight for things that your child needs. For example, the logic of your insurance company's denial of something basic that your child needs is enough to make you want to throw things; or school personnel who are supposed to be helping your child seem to not know them at all and not care.

Many things will be a fight, Situations that used to paralyze you will become part of your day-to-day existence, yet you'll be amazed at the mountains you can move.

No matter how relentless you are, remember that you will not win every battle. Sometimes the answer is just no. Being able to let those things go is important. There will be other wins, better solutions. Even when a defeat seems overwhelming, trust that you're a good advocate and your child can depend on you to provide what they need.

## You may want to consider professional counseling at certain times on this journey

When professionals write about special needs parenting, they often use words like *denial, continuing sadness, depression, guilt, PTSD*, and a myriad of others that try to define what raising a special needs child is like. All these words are appropriate, and sometimes this information is useful. It can help you understand that your feelings are normal. It can reassure you that you're not alone and that others have been where you are and have found ways to thrive.

I'd like to encourage you to be willing to consider professional support. A good therapist can be a life-changing gift you give yourself. Looking for outside help doesn't mean you're weak or that you've failed. It doesn't mean you're not a good parent. It simply means you're willing to use all the tools available so you can live well and be the best parent you can be.

I'm by no means qualified to say who needs what, or how to get what you need. I've done lots of therapy at different times in my life. Some experiences have been better than others, but each time I reached out for counseling support I was given new insights. I was able to look at situations much more clearly and was able to move forward.

## Some people (even family) will deny your child's disability, and blame you

It's sad but true. Denial is a funny thing when it comes to families with special kids. Even people who love you and your child can be so determined to deny that there's anything wrong with them that they blame their disability on parenting. Maybe you've already heard some of these: "If they would let that kid get enough exercise he would be walking by now." "If I had that kid with me for a week she would be talking." "Of course she doesn't talk; she doesn't have to. They give her whatever she wants before she has to ask for it."

Hearing comments like these from people whose judgment you have always trusted makes it hard not to believe you're causing your child's problems. Hearing them from people you were counting on for support can be heartbreaking. But believing them can be deadly!

Remember that people who love you are dealing with their own denial. They love your child and want to find easy answers that fix everything. The most important thing is to stay focused on what's true. Your child's limitations are not your fault. You did not cause them, and you cannot parent them away.

## The most important thing you can teach your special kid is to be independent

Your child needs to be able to trust that no matter what their limitations are, they can be confident in their ability to advocate for themselves. Yet your strongest instinct is to protect them.

It's easy to assume that because of their disability they need more protecting than typical children. The truth is that the ability to try things, no matter how they turn out, can be most important for kids with special needs. Let them start small. Speaking for themselves at a doctor's appointment can be life-changing. Including them in an individual education plan (IEP) meeting can be a first step in helping them learn to manage their own life.

Even when it's scary, invest in helping your child move toward more independence. The benefits of this will ripple throughout their entire life.

## Part of your growth on this journey is letting go of guilt

You can spend hours trying to figure out what you did wrong to make your child have a disability. Even if you know intellectually that that doesn't make sense, your mind can drift back to feeling guilty when you see your child struggle.

The truth is you will never know why this disability happened to your child. What you do know in your deepest heart is that you would never intentionally hurt your precious child. Set aside the guilt and concentrate on trusting you and your child to do whatever you have to do to make their life better.

## Some days you will be truly heartbroken over how difficult things are for your kiddo

No matter how centered you feel or how spiritually aware you think you are, the heartbreak and crushing sadness will be there. Allow it to exist until it lets up. You will hate these days.

What is even harder to watch is when your kid has these days. Some days they will find no peace or acceptance – they're just angry, or sad, or both. They're weary of being different. They're tired of therapy and doctors and your nagging at them to keep working hard.

It's your job to not panic on these days. It's your job to show your child that these days are part of the life they're living. And while you cannot keep these days from happening, you can show them that these feelings don't make them a failure. You can assure them that the feelings will pass.

Are you willing to let your child feel hopeless without guilt? Help them learn that they have the skills they need to not stay stuck there.

## Your job as a parent of a special kid is, at its core, the same as that of any other parent

You are charged to do the best you can to prepare your kid to live in a world that does not embrace them. You are charged with making them as brave as they can be. Your tendency might be to assume that your kiddo needs an extra dose of protection. You might often think that your main job is to shield them from a world that doesn't understand them. But the quality of their life depends largely on their willingness to learn to fend for themselves. They need to understand that trying is much more important than succeeding.

Are you willing to push them beyond their comfort zone and yours? Are you willing to let them try anything they're willing to? Take a good hard look at this – it is and will always be important.

# Hold On; Help Is Coming

Being a special needs parent is not for sissies. It's not easy. Nobody's ever prepared, and nobody expects to be part of this club. The great surprise is that there's an army of people who have been down this road who are ready and willing to help you. All those feelings you're having that there are no words for – somebody else had them too. They don't have the words either but they do know how it feels.

Reaching out and trusting strangers does not come easily for most of us. Do it anyway. You need support even more than you might think you do; and so does your child. One of the greatest gifts you will ever give them is the understanding that asking for help and being willing to let others into their life and their heart is a sign of great strength. Make a conscious choice to not allow disability to isolate you and your family. The only way your special kiddo is going to learn this lesson is if they see you do it.

You, your family, and your special kiddo are about to learn the secrets of a "love language" that sometimes contains no words. You're about to start friendships that will change your world forever. Don't miss this. Fight for it. It's so worth it!

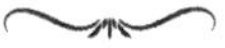

## CHAPTER 2

# Choosing Your Story

The strongest memories I have about the years I was in elementary school are about how I would navigate the world with my disability. Could I do what everybody else was doing? If I couldn't, how was I going to react? Most often my reaction was to seem aloof, unaffected; but I almost never felt that way. I always cared. I was always assessing. Where did I fit? How different was I really? Now I'm not saying I was always miserable; I absolutely was not. I was just busy. Busy figuring out how to best handle the fact that I felt completely different from the whole world.

Some of the coping skills I developed then have turned into my greatest gifts. I was always quick to make jokes about how clumsy I was, or how slow I was. If I made a joke first, it would be harder for anybody else to tease me. Over time I did find humor in it, and I remember how my feelings about it began to change, way back then.

I was probably about eight. As a result, when we meet, I'm likely to make you laugh, at least once or twice.

Even now, at sixty-seven, the feeling of *different* shows up, sometimes at the most unexpected times. No matter how much logic tells me that my CP does not in any way diminish me as a person, there are days when it sure feels like it. There are days when being slower or clumsier is not okay. One of the great heartbreaks of my life is that I could never learn to roller-skate, and I'm still sad about it.

So the feelings are there; they show up. So far I haven't found a way to prevent that from happening. And some days I'm still sad. I'm still self-conscious.

I'm a public speaker, and I really love it. Sometimes I'm really good at it, but I hate walking to the podium. Just about every time I do it, every single step sounds like a gunshot in my head.

So I can't always count on my feelings to match what I know. I decide what my story is even when I hate my CP. I work at it – not every day, but often.

Over the years, deciding what my story is has become my "go to." It gives me the freedom to live my life richly. That will work for you too. You can live richly and help your special kid do the same. I hope some of the entries in this chapter help you consciously decide what your story is going to be.

## You decide what's important and what parts of your history define you

Will you focus on your child having a disability or will you focus on helping them learn what their unique talents are? The answer to this question is always going to be "It depends." Some days the focus has to be on the disability. It's part of what needs to be done. No matter how hectic and busy life gets, it's just as vital to devote time and energy to helping your child discover their own interests and decide what they're passionate about. Like all children, their phases come and go, and their interests change. It doesn't matter. What matters is learning and understanding that you are what you care about. Your gifts are unique and special, and the world needs them. Make the favorite things about yourself your story.

What's the best way to help your child learn to choose their story? Being good at choosing your own. You're more than a parent with a special child.

## Be careful about what you say to other people

Some days I let a few choice things slip out, but as a general rule I can count on myself to be rather civil. I talk with myself much more than I talk to anybody else. There's a conversation going on in my head whenever my mouth isn't moving or I'm not totally engrossed in what's going on around me. The story I hear most often is the one I tell myself, so it has the biggest impact on how I see the world.

It's likely that when your special child was born, the story you told yourself about yourself changed. Their presence in your life directly affected your story.

Pay attention and see if your story is still the one you want to keep repeating.

## For a different perspective, think of the people in your life who think you're special

Imagine the possibilities of your life in the same way your biggest fans do. What do they see that you often overlook? The more you truly learn to celebrate yourself the way your best friends celebrate you, the closer you come to enjoying your life to the fullest.

You might not be sure you can really change what you see, but I know you would like to be able to teach your child to celebrate themselves just the way they are. Learning to do that for yourself is the best shot you have at teaching it to them.

## Can you possibly imagine that your child's disability is a great gift?

Do their limitations give them a chance to see things typical people miss?

Even though it's true that I would much rather be an Olympic athlete than a woman with CP, there have been gifts that came along with my disability. Learning to be patient with myself has taught me patience with others. Learning to love myself when I really wanted to hate parts of what I was living with has taught me compassion. I've learned that all of us live with being different from what we would like to be or intended to be. I think knowing and understanding this one thing has allowed me to experience the great friendships and deep connections I have with the people in my life.

I believe that really knowing the people you love is as close to God as you ever get. Never doubt that there's something wonderful about the unique way your child sees the world.

## You are always making decisions that have serious consequences

Are you strong enough and wise enough to make the best choices? What if you saw yourself as brave and wise and the best person to make decisions for your child? How different would your life be?

Tell yourself the story that deep down you know is true. You're capable of making good decisions in tough situations.

## Your story should be written by you

Be close to the people around you and always be grateful for their support. Let them know how much you value them and that they're gifts to you. But don't let them define your life for you. That job is yours alone. You decide what the events in your life mean, and you decide what's possible.

Those who love you might try to protect you in ways that make you less than what you are. They might want you to do what is easiest. No matter how good their intentions, don't fall for it – not for you, not for your kiddo.

You both are so much stronger than you think.

## Your child can decide what their story is

Sometimes it's so painful to see how hard everyday things can be for your child because they're not typical. Do you believe they're responsible for their own happiness, even if what they face seems impossibly hard? No matter what their circumstances, they still must make the choice about how happy they're willing to be. You cannot make that decision for them.

Are you willing to allow them to decide what their life story is going to be?

## Sometimes it's easy to compare your journey to the journeys of other parents and their families

It's almost impossible to avoid these comparisons. However, it's detrimental to base your story on what you think you see in other families. It's one of the fastest ways to get stuck in fear, guilt, and hopelessness, and it's never helpful. Build your own story based on your special talents and dreams. You're the perfect person to be living your life. You're in exactly the place you're supposed to be today.

## Finding joy separate from your child is necessary to create a complete story

You know this is true. When you have a child with special needs it can be much harder for you to take the time to do something for the sheer joy of it. There always seems to be something that needs doing.

Plan to set aside time to do something you love. What does that plan look like? What's on your list of things you would love to make part of your life?

## Make conscious choices about the story you tell yourself about your child

You may find yourself thinking about your child in unrealistic ways. You might think of them as "my hero" or "God's way to teach me to be more patient or more compassionate."

Applaud the amazing bravery you see when they fight to accomplish something new. Even so, find a way in your story to remember that they're just a kid. They have a right to be ordinary. Because sometimes they can be a brat. Some days they can be lazy. All kids are! It's not fair to put pressure on them to be bigger than life every day.

## The only story you have any control over is your own

Your story is not just about outcomes or results. Your story is also about how you see yourself in the world, how you react to your life, and the relationships you build with the people around you. Whether it's one of the days when you're positive you cannot do this one more day, or one when something marvelous happens, both are part of your story. On either day, remember to talk to yourself with love and respect.

## Some days you miss the person you were before your special kid was born

You miss the days when you didn't have to plan life around therapy appointments and doctor visits. However, it's easy to forget that all parents have fond memories of their pre-parent days. Some of those memories are real, but it's likely that some of those times weren't as great as you remember. Sometimes you look back and grieve what was, but be gentle with yourself when you go back to that place in your mind. It's just as much a part of your story as this time is. Allow that sweet sadness to find its place in your heart and push forward.

## Convincing yourself that your child's disability is not your fault

Even when logic or medical facts should be enough to convince you that your guilt makes no sense, you can still get stuck in blaming yourself. *Really* stuck.

Sometimes the guilt is so heavy and pervasive that you feel paralyzed. But guilt is a luxury you cannot afford. It does nothing to help you take better care of your kiddo. It does nothing to help you get closer to the story you want to tell yourself. You can decide today that you will not give guilt enough of your energy to have it interfere with your story.

## Take time today to give a voice to what you're good at

Give yourself credit for what you do best. Some days you're an exceptional problem-solver. Some days you can negotiate as well as anybody in the United Nations. Maybe you're an artist, or a writer. Let yourself focus on the ways you make the world better. Honor the talents you have and give voice to them today. The more comfortable you are with owning and celebrating your gifts and talents, the easier it is to help make the world better. Teaching your child to celebrate their own gifts improves their life in ways you cannot even imagine.

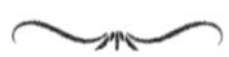

## Forgiveness is a major part of the best story you can tell yourself

There are a lot of things you have a right to be angry at. Nothing about any of this is fair. Your beautiful child certainly does not deserve to have such a hard road to travel. People aren't fair to your child. The world is full of people and situations that hurt them, and people often don't know any better.

You'll keep learning to be a better advocate all the time. You'll continue to speak up for your child in the most effective way possible. Do what you can, then let the rest go. Nobody and no situation is important enough for you to give up your joy. Forgive as soon as you can, simply because you deserve it. Forgiveness is a gift you give to yourself.

## You want the story you tell yourself to be based in courage

Take time to think of one thing you would do if you were not afraid. Talk about this thing to the people in your life and pay close attention to how they react. They likely don't think it's nearly as impossible as it seems to you. You can get better and better at this with practice.

If you wait for your fear to go away, changes will probably never happen. So plan to move forward and do it. Your special child will need to be far more courageous than you are. You cannot help them achieve bravery by telling them to be brave, but you can help them learn to be brave by living bravely yourself.

## Choose to be relaxed and don't obsess over things you have no control over

You have so many reasons to be in a state of panic, but you can make another choice. Make another choice for you and for your child. Like most things that matter, this takes practice.

I invite you, this very minute, to practice relaxing and then understand that there are some things in this world you'll never have control over. No matter what's happening, in this *minute*, you're *fine*. It's only when you look beyond the present moment and into the future that worry takes over.

Make a commitment to focus on the present moment. This choice can permanently alter your story.

## YOU'RE EXTREMELY LUCKY TO HAVE SO MUCH INFORMATION AVAILABLE ABOUT OPTIONS FOR YOUR SPECIAL KIDDO

It's your choice to believe otherwise. Choose your story.

You have access to an amazing medical community, and you can contact other families who are walking the same path. It's hard to imagine getting through your life without all these kinds of support. The problem comes when you must get through all the noise in your head and decide what to integrate.

All this information helps you the most when you get comfortable being able to say, "I don't know," or "It sounds great [or exciting or promising], but I'm still not sure what I think." This is a hard place to be because you want answers. You want concrete solutions.

But the truth is you don't know what's best to do until you know. You can relax in the period of not knowing to keep your internal voice peaceful.

## One of the hardest things about raising a special child is that it can be so lonely

You can feel cut off from the entire world. Nobody understands how you feel. People who love you and love your child often say things that are hurtful. On some level you know they don't mean to, but that doesn't make it hurt less.

Other special needs families can provide you with the support you need, and they're exactly what you need. However, these relationships can get complicated. You might not relate well with a family whose child is at a different level of disability than yours. A split might occur between your family and one that chooses a particular type of therapy or treatment that your family doesn't support. Sometimes a split occurs between families or groups with differing religious or spiritual beliefs.

Finding a place for you and your family in the special needs community is vital to your story. Since you're all dealing with serious emotional issues with serious consequences, misunderstandings happen easily. Remember to love much and judge little. Be quiet instead of critical. When you share with others who also have special children, focus on how you make them feel rather than what you think they should do and how right you are.

## THE STORY YOU TELL YOURSELF IS AFFECTED BY HOW PEOPLE REACT TO YOUR CHILD

When you meet strangers in public and you just know they're about to make a comment or ask a question, it can make you a little nervous. Without meaning to, they can say something that sounds innocent but makes you angry.

For example, something as simple as "She looks tired" can elicit unexpected anger. You know your daughter is not tired. She checked out because she's on overload. Or she's not making eye contact because she's trying to listen to what's going on around her.

Every time this happens you have to decide how you're going to react. Do you offer some education or explanation? Some days you might, if you like the way you feel around this person and are having a pretty good day. Most often you just say, "Yeah, we've had a busy day." How you respond may not matter at all. What matters is how you're going to feel about it two hours from now. Will it still be on your mind and will you still be angry?

That's the part of the interaction you really have control over. No matter how people react to you, you have a choice about how they affect your story.

## When people love you and are comfortable with your child, you know it

You can see it in how they look at you and how they watch your child. They're comfortable asking questions or listening when you talk about whatever the issue of the day is. They also see you as much more than a parent with a special needs child. Stick with those people. Let them be the ones who help you write your story.

There are people who love you and want to be part of your life, but they can't quite get there. Maybe you don't know exactly why, but you can feel that your child makes them uncomfortable. It's okay to let them go. You don't have to fix them or try to make things easy for them. You don't have to make big proclamations. You don't even have to be angry. Just know that whatever it is that makes them uncomfortable is not your fault. Let them go with as much love and forgiveness as you can muster.

## The human spirit is an amazing thing

Your child is far more capable than you think. No matter how they communicate, how they move, or what they seem to understand, they're a child of the Universe. Because you love them and they've been put in your care, you'll be an important part of shaping who they are.

An important part of your story is that you do the best you can on any given day. But the outcome is not yours to decide. You can choose to have a peaceful heart, knowing that your child is writing their own story the way it was meant to be written.

**If you could talk to the person you were on the day you found out you had a special needs child, you would tell yourself, "Things are going to be okay. Most of the things you're worrying about will never happen"**

You would also say, "You're much stronger and wiser than you think, so relax."

You've survived things you never thought you could and found love you never knew existed along the way, so the wonderful thing is that you can say those things to your future self as well.

## CHAPTER 3

# Begin Again

I love the idea that you can decide to begin again – kind of like getting a do-over. Starting again won't be perfect. I'm still me – still sometimes awesome, and still sometimes crazy as a loon – but I have the strength and knowledge I earned from surviving this far. And so do you.

I hope some of these readings on beginning again help you find a bit more joy, quiet, and confidence. My guess is that some will. Enjoy those; maybe even bookmark them to come back to on another day. Some will make no sense at all and may not apply to anything that matters to you. Forget those; don't overthink it.

Remember that you're just fine and getting better all the time.

## When you make a new beginning, the best place to start is right where you are

Whatever you're feeling today is just fine. Today, be as honest as you can with yourself about how you feel about your child and your life. Realize that your feelings do not have to control your behavior or your attitude. Feelings only have control over you when you cannot accept what they are.

No matter what, trust that you will know what to do for your child when it's time to know. You're their best possible parent.

## There will always be a difference between the parent you want to be and the one you are

Most days you're too busy or too tired to think about how big the gap is. Some days you're amazed by how close you come to parenting exactly the way you want to. Love and appreciate those days. Some days the gap between the two seems so big that you feel like a failure. Treat yourself very gently on those days.

You're much better at this than you think. Realize that you, like your child, are a work in progress. Imagine what you would say to your very best friend if they were raising your child. Say that in your head. Over and over.

You, my friend, are *amazing*.

## You would love to be able to take your child's disability away, or to heal it

Wishing you could will always be part of your life, but be careful how much time and energy you give those thoughts. I found that when I spend too much time trying to wish away my cerebral palsy, I can get stuck in self-pity. Even a little bit of self-pity goes a long way in the wrong direction.

I can't change what is; neither can you. I can't even change the fact that some days I really hate having any limitations; neither can you.

What I can change is how I'm going to react today. So can you. Decide today whether you will focus on what your child can do or what they can't do.

## You have the power to control your reactions to how people treat your child

Sometimes you watch people stare and are amazed at how angry you can get. You see your child's feelings get hurt when they're left out. A birthday party invitation does not come and the heart of the person you love most is broken. I hate that this is true, but it's likely that something like this will happen to your child. It happened to me. It happened to my parents. I survived it, and so did they. The people who truly loved us and were meant to be in our lives showed up and stayed. Your people will show up too.

The ways people react to your child have nothing to do with your child. They come from their own experiences. You have no power to change others' reactions. What you can do is make it as easy as possible for them to get to know your child. Welcome questions. Be willing to expose your kiddo to as many environments as you can. As people get to know your child they will begin to see all the wonderful things you see in them.

## Make a commitment to feeling more joy

Concentrate on finding more joy, regardless of your current circumstances. One of the most dangerous things to do is to allow your joy to be dependent on your child's. It's not fair to you and puts an unrealistic burden on your child. Tell yourself that today you will remind yourself that your happiness is your responsibility. What will you do today to find some moments of joy?

## Sometimes it's amazing how crazy things get in your head

It can seem like you have a committee of voices rattling around up there whose personal mission it is to convince you that everything is awful and it's only going to get worse. You might even think to yourself, "My child is never going to be happy and neither am I." The easiest way to quiet the crazy voices is to focus on today – just today. And even sometimes that's too much. Try focusing on the next five minutes.

This is something you can do. You can be present for your child today.

## There are so many wonderful things about your child

There are things this kiddo does better than anybody else! Notice how unique and special your child is. One of the gifts of focusing on the present is that you won't miss the tiny, wonderful things about your kid and the gifts they bring to your life and the lives of the people around them. Pay closer attention to these things and be sure your child knows that you notice their gifts.

## YOU WILL MEET SO MANY WONDERFUL PEOPLE

You cannot imagine your life without many of them. When you need answers you don't have you begin to think that you're not going to meet any other great people who will be able to help you. You can feel alone and isolated. This is *never* the truth. The next person you need always shows up if you're open and willing to listen.

## Making Hard Decisions

Sometimes the consequences of your decisions seem so catastrophic that you feel paralyzed. What makes it even harder is that when people are genuinely trying to help you, it's easy to be overly defensive or protective. If you let fear or your ego get in the way, you can totally miss what might be helpful or even life-changing suggestions.

Let yourself get quieter inside when people are trying to help. You might not decide to follow the recommendations they make, but work on being relaxed and trusting enough to really hear what their suggestions are.

## "I hate feelings; I really do"

The biggest problem with feelings is they don't make sense. The second biggest problem is that if you don't acknowledge them, or refuse to identify them, they inevitably show up and you find yourself doing or saying things you regret.

But feelings don't have to affect your behavior. If you've been up all night with a kid in pain or too upset to sleep, and you're so tired you can't think, there's a good chance you're angry at God or the Universe or whoever's idea this was. You might want to really let somebody have it or give a doctor or a teacher a real piece of your mind. Just because you really feel like that today doesn't mean you have to blow up at anybody. It might be a better idea to take a nap or run around the block – anything to give you a little time to think before you speak. My experience is that it's much easier to stay quiet than to have to apologize to people I don't particularly like.

## The real you is a good person

In a general sense, I'm a very nice person. Most people seem to think so, and I'm lucky that people I love make me feel important. It's hard to understand how a person as nice as I am can feel the ugly feelings that I do sometimes. Sometimes I'm jealous of my friends who have typical bodies. What makes me angry might be something as simple as watching somebody bend over and pick up something without a second thought. My first inclination is to deny that I ever feel like this. After all, since I've written a book about this stuff I must have gotten completely over this by now. But there it is.... Every now and then I'm just angry. It's not fair.

As I get more and more practice accepting all my feelings, it's easier to realize that the *real* me is a good person. My life is not an act.

So if you see people staring at your kid and wish you could think of something to say that would make them feel just awful, don't panic. If you look at your kid on a really hard day and just don't want to deal with it any more, it doesn't mean you're an awful person or that you don't love your child. It means you're human; that you're a real person with real feelings who loves to the depths of your soul. It means your life is not an act.

Give yourself the freedom to look at your scariest feelings – to admit to yourself that they're there.

## People you love can get you through the toughest times

Other times the way people react to you can break your heart or make you angry enough to throw things. And you can never tell for sure which people are going to end up in which group. If this journey is very new to you, you might be surprised when someone you expected to be an ongoing part of your life just sort of disappears, while someone you never expected to be there is and continues to be.

Let people be who they are. Don't waste energy being angry or hurt by people who choose to step away from you because of your child. Spend your energy being grateful for the folks who are there for you.

## People often say the dumbest things about your life or your child

They might say, "You're so brave, I absolutely could not do what you do."

"Really?" you think to yourself. "What would you do instead? Throw your kid away? Run away screaming into the sunset?"

What I think they're really saying is, "I'm so grateful I don't have a kid like yours, and I need to believe that I'm different from you. If we're different enough, I can be sure that what has happened to you could never happen to me."

In a lot of ways, the life you lead every day – with all the ups and downs, the tough times, and the moments of such great joy – is another parent's worst nightmare. There will always be times when seeing you makes someone reflect on that which they dread most. They say dumb things, and sometimes hurtful things, without even realizing it.

When this happens, let it go. Even when these kinds of statements sting, it really has nothing to do with you.

## Some people will instantly bond with your special child

There are others who have become important to you over time, and they're wonderful. Some days you cannot imagine how you could get along without them, even though there are times you tend to push them away or even get angry at them for no apparent reason, just in case they decide to back away. It seems like you can never find a way to pay them back for all they do for you.

I know I've pushed people away because it frightened me to think about how much I needed them. Sometimes I've been able to mend the relationships and sometimes not.

You have the ability to stop and change course when you feel yourself pushing people away because you're afraid you'll lose them. Think about how much they really mean to you or to your child.

## This may not be what you had in mind

Sometimes the life you're leading has its own rewards and it's hard to believe how much joy it's bringing you. Cherish those days. Other days you can get stuck in the "what might have beens" or the "if onlys."

You're always going to wish the life of your child was an easier one. However, dwelling on how your lives could have been without the disability can leave you stuck and drain your energy. Even on the days when you find yourself wishing things were different, realize that staying stuck in regret zaps your energy and makes you miss the joy in your life today.

I think you probably have an idea in your head about what you should be able to do for your child. Your patience should be endless. The ideas for solving problems should come to you by the thousands, and always work better than you ever could have imagined. In this magic world that lives in your head, you can instantly make your child feel better if they're discouraged. In fact, you're such an amazing parent that your child is doing amazing things every single day. You're convinced that the Lifetime Channel will be at your house any day to film your heartwarming story.

Some of your best ideas can come from this magical and make-believe place. But you do not live there. The reality of what you can do is not perfect. It's simply the best you can do on any given day.

## Make this your favorite question: "What would I do if I were not afraid?"

Consider this for your child: What would I wish for my kiddo if I were not afraid? What if I were not afraid they would get hurt or laughed at? What would I encourage them to do if I were not afraid that if they tried something and failed, they might not have the nerve to try again?

The more your child is willing to try things, the richer their life will be. The greatest gift you might ever give them is the understanding that trying is much more important than succeeding. They need to know that trying one thing can lead to succeeding in something else altogether, and that "something else" might be far greater than their original goal.

## YOU PROBABLY CAN'T THINK OF A TIME WHEN YOU SAID TO YOURSELF "THIS IS BRAVE"

What you do remember is feeling so scared that you wanted to crawl into a hole. But you can think of lots of times when you were that scared and moved your feet forward anyway. Courage is doing and deciding, when your fear is telling you to "Do nothing and hide."

Think of yourself as courageous every time you move past fear. Learn to trust that you'll be brave enough to do the best you can and make the best possible decisions, even when you're afraid.

## Your child can navigate the world with courage and grace

If you could trade places with your special child, how would you do? Could you accept life with a disability? As close as you are to them, and as much time as you spend with them, you have no idea what it really feels like to be them. You cannot know what it's really like to have a body or a mind that makes you different from most of the world.

If you really would like to know more about what your child feels, ask them; and take the time to listen, or if they communicate differently, to watch more closely. Make sure they know you respect them for the courage it takes to live their life every day. Make sure they know that their disability is not a taboo subject.

Talk openly with your special kid about all aspects of their disability.

## Advocating for your child may be the single most important thing you do for them

You're often the link between your child and a world that doesn't understand them or is afraid of them. It's easy to be so protective and so angry with anybody who might hurt them that you're too quick to judge, and treat people unfairly. As a result, people might not want to have much to do with your child because you're hard to deal with.

Figuring out when to be protective and when to trust the world to be fair is always tricky. You can't get it right all the time. But your instincts are good. Trust them. Be willing to be gentle with the parts of the world that want to embrace and support your child.

## Decide what will make your journey with your child more wonderful; then do more of that

Work on self-discovery with kindness. Simply let go of things that aren't working for your child. Understand that all the decisions you've made so far have been the best decisions you could have made at the time.

Commit to examining your life through eyes of love. Show yourself the same kindness you show other people you love.

## LONG BEFORE YOU HAD CHILDREN YOU HAD IDEAS ABOUT HOW THE WORLD WAS SUPPOSED TO WORK. YOU THOUGHT FOR SURE YOU KNEW THE DIFFERENCE BETWEEN GOOD AND BAD AND RIGHT AND WRONG

As your child grows and new awareness comes to you, what you believe to be true and false and right and wrong is shifting. Be willing to examine your beliefs to make sure they still work in your life today. Trust yourself to rethink old ideas. You know more now than you ever did before, and in some areas you're wiser.

I wish for you courage and freedom to allow yourself to change the way you think and what you believe.

## You do not need to control every detail of your child's care

The problem with this approach is that you're not the only one with a brain. Your way is never the *only* way. In fact, it may or may not be the best way.

When you let go of control, it's easier to work with others as a team, and almost always results in the very best outcomes for your child.

Be more conscious of your need to control all the details. Trust that the ideas of the whole team are often better than your ideas alone.

## You still need the fun stuff!

If you and your child are facing a big issue, it's easy to convince yourself that all things you do for pleasure must go by the wayside. You might give up regular meetings with friends because you're needed at home. Hobbies you love or teams you belong to may be neglected.

These are things that feed you and bring you joy. You cannot give your child, or anybody else, what you don't have. People who depend on you also depend on your taking good care of yourself.

## Your spiritual condition matters

Frankly, this idea scares me to death. When I'm stressed or overtired, spirituality is usually the last thing on my mind.

Spiritual growth doesn't mean you need to know all the answers or have an inside view of some master plan. You just need to be exactly where you are and be willing to change the way you see the world if what makes sense starts to change. Be willing to have a deeper understanding of your spiritual connection to the Universe.

Sometimes all you can do is just be willing to be willing. Are you willing to allow yourself to grow spiritually today?

## You read a lot to find information to help your child

You're always looking for the latest research. It's important to do the best you can to educate yourself, but your response to the world, and to life with your child, is uniquely yours.

You can read and learn and try things. Some will work. Some won't. It doesn't matter. Trust that you will always be the best final decider for your kiddo.

## It can feel like you will hurt forever

Peace and happiness seem to be gone forever. Forgotten is the fact that problems like this have been faced and conquered in the past.

Struggles from the past might not have direct bearing on what you face today, but you know that you overcame them before and it made you stronger. Even if the problems you face today are bigger than any you have faced before, so is your ability to handle them. This journey is making you a much stronger person. Learn to count on this strength when you need it.

## The greatest resources you have are within you

If you're still and quiet and don't panic, the answers you need will come. Even when you're terrified, the answers will come.

You don't have to react or respond to every thought or feeling you have. The more you're willing to do what is in front of you to do, the stronger you become. When you're afraid, practice becoming still and quiet and trust that your best solutions come from what you already know.

## You have so many blessings to be grateful for

Be grateful for the professionals who are dedicated to your child and have been able to help them do miraculous things. Be most grateful for the beautiful child you've been given. Watching them grow into the best person they can be, with more courage than you can begin to understand, has added richness to your life that you didn't think was possible.

## Be grateful today for your own journey

Be grateful for the changes in yourself that let you know you're growing. Be grateful that you're learning to forgive yourself for the mistakes you make. You know that you are and always will be "a work in progress." You're learning that perfection is not possible.

The world is better because you're in it, and you're the perfect parent for your child. Focus on enjoying the trip. You're willing to allow the changes in yourself to continue, and you'll be patient when growth seems impossibly slow. You'll take note and rejoice when you see the changes in yourself that are truly amazing.

# CHAPTER 4

# Trust Me, You're Doing Great!

Feeling different from everybody else has always made me lonely. I feel differently about my CP than I want to; not every day, but sometimes – at least more often than I want you to know. Yes, I know that I "shouldn't" be embarrassed about how I feel about it. But what I know and what I feel don't always match. No matter what my feelings are, I'm not a pathetic failure. I don't hate myself. I'm not whining; I'm being human.

Life with your kiddo is often lonely. Acceptance and peace come in spurts, not all at once and not permanently. Any feeling you have on any given day is just as it should be. Hold on to the ones that serve you well, and let the others go.

There's a whole community of us who want to hold you up, just as you are. We may not have words for all your feelings either, but we have felt them. You're not unique; you're one of us. Find us. Our journeys are not identical, but we're all moving in the same direction.

## People are not always predictable

Disability frightens some people. Others are so uncomfortable that it doesn't seem worth it to continue a relationship with them.

Some people who moved out of your life have been devastating losses. You need to consciously decide to let them go at least a hundred times. That's okay. Do it as many times as it takes.

Some have slipped away without much notice. Some who you never expected to, have become important people in your support system.

How others react to the reality of your life today has *nothing* to do with you or your child. If they need to step away, let them go with love. Realize that their reactions come from their own story, not yours. Maybe they'll be back; maybe not. You're not responsible for that. What you are responsible for is being willing to let go of people who cannot find a place in your life. Let people go, having faith that those you need will show up.

## When you have a child with a disability it can be hard to make sense of your feelings

You're positive that your feelings are not what they should be. You should be more grateful or accepting. You should certainly be less envious of your friends and their children.

There seem to be two versions of your life. There's the public version, the one people say is inspiring. "You're so strong," they say. "You are so brave." Then there's this other, private version. You can get so angry. So tired. You get stuck in how unfair it all is. Even things you thought you accepted long ago can make you feel like you're absolutely on the edge of crazy.

There's a little bit of you in both versions. Some days you really do love this life. Raising this child has made you a far better person. You have a deeply spiritual connection that surprises you every day. Many people you've met because of your child are truly blessings. You're so grateful for them, and without your kiddo you probably would have missed them. Other days you're bitter, angry, scared.

Peace comes when you know that both sets of feelings are fine. Please have the courage to honor both and know that the best you can do on any given day is enough.

## You worry incessantly about your child's future

Some of your concerns are real. Sometimes good options for people with your child's disability can be hard to find. Trust that when it's time you'll be able to help them make a good plan.

Today, focus on helping them develop the skills they'll need to live well. That's the best future you'll ever be able to give them.

Please do the best you can today to release your worries about your child's future.

## You are torn between encouraging your child to try new things and protecting them

You watch your child running full steam toward what seems to be a brick wall. You feel like screaming "STOP!" and they run faster.

On another day you see kids doing something that you're sure would be good for your child, but your child has no interest in it or they're too scared to try it. The odd part is that you never quite know which kid is going to show up on any given day.

It doesn't matter. Your job is always to encourage them no matter what. You may not know which is a brick wall and which is a launching pad, and it's not your business to figure that out. It's your business to teach them that trying is what matters, and success is a bonus.

Your child needs to have enough faith in themselves to try whatever interests them. They need to know that they will survive whatever the outcome happens to be.

## Find other special needs families

You meet each other at support groups, school activities, doctors' offices. Before long you begin to wonder how in the world you got along without each other. Often these families become much more like family than people who are related to you.

When you get busy and it feels like all you can possibly do is survive, it can seem like it's too much work to make time for others who are walking the same path. When you feel yourself falling into that way of thinking, take it as a warning sign that you're beginning to isolate yourself. Isolation is deadly. You need others around you who can give you honest feedback. You need people you can talk to in "shorthand" and they get it.

## It's easy to be defensive about your special kid

You want to always be open and willing to accept support offered to you. You want to be able to embrace innovative ideas that will be game-changers and move your kid forward. However, there have been enough times when people said and did hurtful things that you tend to head into new situations ready to pounce.

The reality is that the world does not understand your child. People make assumptions about them that are clearly not true. It is often up to you to educate others and make your child's path easier. Sometimes that means standing up to people who don't agree with you.

This is never easy, and striking the right balance is a lifelong learning process. Keep learning to be a strong advocate and remain open enough to be approachable. Your instincts are much better than you think.

## What you want from people in your life is encouragement

You want them to look past what your kid can't do and see how amazing and determined they are. Choose to believe that people are doing the best they can. The idea of having a child with the struggles your child has is unimaginably horrible to most parents. It might take them some time to get past those feelings to be able to see possibilities for your family.

Cut the people around you a little slack. Share successes and be willing to show others how proud you are of your wonderful kiddo. Keep learning to accept people right where they are.

## Your most constant battle is with your own feelings; and your child's is too

It seems like you're always trying to accept your feelings, understand them, celebrate them, communicate them, or deny them.

Your child's struggle is the same. You cannot protect them from the pain of coming to terms with life with a disability. You have some ideas about how they must feel, but accept right now, and over and over again, that you don't really know. All you can do is give them a safe space in which to figure out their own path to acceptance and peace. Trust that they can find their own way to a joyful, meaningful life.

The process for your child to find acceptance is no easier than yours. It's a lifelong journey for them too. And it's messy. It's painful and sometimes scary and ugly. It's also beautiful, and they'll receive a closer look at love than most people ever get to experience.

You don't have all the answers. You don't even know all the questions. Just be there. Allow your child to walk this journey their way. Help them understand that all their feelings are okay.

## There's a picture in your mind of what you should be like as a parent

There is also a picture in your mind of what you *really are* as a parent. Neither one of these pictures is accurate. What you think you should be able to do is clearly not reality and you don't give yourself credit for all the things you should feel good about. Even parents of typical kids get caught up in guilt that they struggle to let go of.

Give yourself credit for how far you've come. Give yourself credit for the doctor appointments you went to when they were the last thing in the world you wanted to do. Remember all the battles you've fought and won! All the crises you've lived through. All the times you've advocated for your kid and bucked systems that weren't designed to include them. Celebrate that you've done things you never ever thought you could do.

You did what was needed. You've done so repeatedly. You can be confident that you'll do so again.

## Look at your kiddo as though they're the only kid on the planet

It's a silly thought, but sometimes this outlook is a surprising way to really see how perfect your child is.

Without even realizing it, you most often compare your kid to someone else. You might compare them to others in their class or others who go to the same therapist. Sometimes you even measure them against goals you set, or the desired outcome of a treatment or surgery.

Today, take the time to look at your child just as they are. To communicate with them, however you do that. No matter how busy you are, for just a few minutes see just exactly who they are today.

What could you see in your kid if you had absolutely nothing to compare them to?

## Living with a disability is not easy. It certainly is not a road you would choose for your child

Your love and support are important and certainly make it easier, but there's nothing you can do to take away the challenge that's ahead for the person you love most in the world. The good news is you don't have to. That's not your job. Your job is to help your child not be afraid of their own feelings.

Your child lives their life with a body or a mind that doesn't do what they want it to do. It's hard, and some days they're going to be angry. Some days they're going to be so jealous of everybody who seems normal that it appears they will feel sorry for themselves forever.

They won't, but they wouldn't be human if they didn't sometimes feel like they couldn't make it. Assure them that their feelings are temporary and normal. Their hard days are theirs. It doesn't mean you're not a good parent. It doesn't mean you're not giving them the tools they need. It just means that what they're doing is hard and they're finding their way.

## One thing you can count on is that you will often feel helpless

But of course you're not. You have or will develop skills that, at some point in your life, you had no idea you would ever possess. One day you'll realize you've become an expert on the disability that affects your child. You'll be even better at negotiating systems that aren't easy to navigate. Standing your ground and being heard when people aren't inclined to listen will become a normal part of your day.

Love for your child will move you forward even when progress seems impossible. You'll amaze yourself. You're part of one of the most ferocious groups of people on this planet.

Put one foot in front of the other and do the best you can today. That is enough. You are a force to be reckoned with.

## You're different now than you were then – but the diagnosis hasn't changed

No matter how long it's been since you first realized you were going to be walking this unexpected path, you're different than you were that first day. Some of the changes are obvious and you can look back and smile at what you thought then. Some of them you cannot see but the people in your life certainly can. And some of them you won't even realize have happened until you watch yourself do things you never thought you could.

Realize the changes in you are real. You probably have a few emotional scars that came along with hard-learned lessons. But the changes are happening in you regardless of changes in your child. Even on the toughest days you can trust that you'll continue to grow and evolve.

However you feel today, you're enough. You're the best possible champion for your child.

## Even on the toughest days you know you're better because of your child

I've heard so many people say, "I know my special kiddo has made me a better person." I think this is true for all of you. My cerebral palsy has given me some gifts for sure. But don't expect yourself to become a saint. Don't interpret it to mean that you must develop unwavering patience or that you're not supposed to be tired, angry, or frustrated.

There will be times when you notice you're more compassionate than you were before and that small victories mean much more. When you watch your kiddo work as hard as they can to be the best they can be, it feels like your heart is about to burst, you love them so much. Things that used to seem vitally important matter less. The relationships you build with people who support you and love your child are some of the best you'll ever have. A simple good day can make you giddy.

All these things will happen. Just remember you don't have to make them happen – they just do.

Sometimes they come quickly, sometimes they come slowly, but they will happen if you keep showing up every day.

## THE PAIN OF TODAY CAN MAKE YOU FEEL LIKE YOU WON'T SURVIVE

For some families there are periods of great pain – of fear that seems impossible to survive. No matter what situation you're in, this kind of pain is never permanent. It changes; it always does.

On the awful days – ones that make you realize your life is changing forever – remember that even days like this are *just one day*. In the darkest moments you're introduced to the strongest you. So allow yourself to feel whatever it is. Let yourself sob uncontrollably if that happens. Your feelings, no matter how scary, are just that – feelings. Don't be afraid to feel them. You won't break. Trust yourself even when doing so makes no sense.

## This life gives you amazing moments of terrible clarity

Living with your special kid is a messy process. I don't mean your dishes aren't done or your house is in disarray; I mean you'll feel and think things you never imagined you could. There are days you're beyond sad. You might look at your best friend one day and be furious that you're on your way to therapy and they're headed to gymnastics. You may have to face the fact that you said something, just because it felt unfair, that you knew made her feel badly. You may need to own it and apologize.

There are countless times when I fall short of the kind of person I want to be. I'm sure it's part of the human condition, but those of us who live with and around special needs do have an extra level of stress; there's another layer of issues that affect everything. You have two choices: One, you can accept that these moments of terrible clarity happen and that you sometimes need to forgive yourself; and two, you can pretend they don't happen and wonder why you feel stuck. The choice is always yours.

## I cannot act or treat my child's disability away

I'm forever amazed by how much you know about the conditions that affect your children. I can't tell you how much I've learned over the years about CP from parents. When it comes to learning and reading and researching the next new thing, you're rock stars. The hours you put in going back and forth to appointments, the IEP meetings you attend – all of it is mind-blowing. If you could run the world, I'm convinced we would all be *so* much better off. I love this about you. You're forces to be reckoned with. Do what you do and fight on.

Progress will happen. Goals will be met and surpassed. Kiddos will grow and may achieve things you never imagined. Enjoy and celebrate all of that. For most of us, though, the disability is not going away. It will always be some part of who your kiddo is. It's not your job to cure it. Your child doesn't need to be "normal" to have a joyful life.

## Not having the power to fix your kiddo is one of the hardest parts of your life with them

You watch them be frustrated or disappointed about what they can't do, and your sadness can be devastating. As hard as their struggles are to watch, keep encouraging them to try. Being willing to try is vital to their survival; success is a bonus.

Your instinct might be to protect them from feeling defeated. Make a conscious effort to switch your focus to helping them learn that trying matters much more than succeeding. Willingness to try what seems impossible is the only way to live a life filled with miracles.

## There's nothing you can't accept for just five minutes, even on the worst days

There's no joy that's not made sweeter by focusing all your attention on this exact moment. Learning to stay in the present is a choice. It's a skill that you get better at with practice.

What the future holds for your special child can be your greatest fear. Focusing on it is deadly. Spending time and energy worrying about what's ahead will teach both of you to be afraid. It will zap your energy. Trust that when the time comes you'll be able to make a good long-term plan. For today, the future is not your business.

## Having a special needs child has changed your relationships

There are those who have stepped up and become rocks of your existence. Cherish them. It's also true that some people who used to seem like soul mates have gradually turned into people who don't really understand your life. You find yourself being careful about what you say around these old friends. At times you feel isolated and alone.

The only way to make peace with this is to accept people where they are. Their reactions to you or your child have nothing to do with you. You cannot change what other people think or feel. What you can change is your reaction to them. You can decide how much power to give to them to hurt you.

You can let go of people who aren't good for you right now. This makes more room in your life for the wonderful people who are there to support you.

## Some days you're amazed by how quickly you can get angry

How odd the things are that make me angry! Somebody cuts me off in traffic and I see red. A man in the grocery store sends me to the wrong aisle to look for the bread and I feel rage. When this happens it can feel like something or somebody has taken over my body. The IQ of everybody around me seems to drop thirty points at least. And I can easily convince myself that my anger is okay because my life is so hard.

I guess having a special kiddo can be much the same. It can feel like it gives you permission to be unkind or to say hurtful things. After all, anyone who must do what you do every day has a right to be grumpy. But what's going on with you doesn't have anything at all to do with inconsiderate drivers or incompetent store employees. Your anger is yours and you're one hundred percent responsible for how much it affects your words and your actions. This is true for all of us.

Take time to check in with yourself. Sometimes just focusing on your truth can help change your mood. Sometimes in the "heat of battle" all you can do is decide that this is a good day to keep your mouth shut. Sometimes the best you can do is nothing.

Even if you cannot do anything to change what's going on in the moment, you can control what you say. No matter what, you have control over what comes out of your mouth and how you choose to treat others. Take responsibility for your actions even if you're angry, and don't use your child to excuse unkind behavior.

## You want your child to know that they're loveable just the way they are

The extent to which your child can see this has a profound effect on their happiness. You cannot teach them self-love if you don't love yourself. Developing self-love is a choice and takes work. Mastering it is a lifelong pursuit. Be conscious today of how important it is to be gentle and loving to yourself. Find ways to model this for your child. Talk to them about how you learned self-love and what you think about it.

## When you wake up you're never sure what kind of a day it's going to be

Your day can go south at any given moment. Your child's health can turn on a dime. Your day can go from ordinary to a crisis at any time.

I've learned to think of something positive when I wake up. It only takes a second and can give you the extra boost you may need to face what's going to happen in your life that day. It hasn't been an easy habit to develop, and you might have to really work at it. It's so much easier to start your day with a sense of dread, especially if you're overtired (which is probably most of the time). Be positive anyway. In the beginning you might feel a little silly, but make yourself start the day with a positive thought. Any morning that you forget, do it as soon as you remember. Do this until it becomes automatic.

Then help your child do the same. Show them that they have some control over what they think about every day. Teach them that starting the day with a positive thought is always helpful.

## Comparisons are deadly. When you feel one coming on, Stop it!

No matter how much you know in your head that this is not helpful, you will do it anyway. We are all much too human not to fall into this trap sometimes.

Pay attention to what you're thinking, and when you realize you're comparing yourself or your child to somebody else, switch your focus. If a family is doing something that looks like it might be helpful to your child, be willing to ask questions. Ask for suggestions. Is it something you can do?

Be happy for the progress of other kids. If you're impressed by something you see another parent doing, tell them so. They need encouragement as much as you do.

If you want suggestions about something that works for somebody else, ask. Switching focus to a more useful point of view is something you can do, but it has nothing to do with anybody else.

## You want to believe that the people in your child's life really want to support them

You want to believe that they can see past your child's disability in the same way you can; that they take the time to see them as the magic little person you see. You want to believe that your child's peers will work hard to include them and that their teachers are committed to helping them learn in ways that work for them. You want to believe that the world you're helping to build for your child will always be a safe one.

In spite of how much you want this safety for your child, some of your experiences have been far different from that. People you loved and trusted have let you down. People have hurt your child's feelings over and over. Even so, you want to stay open. You want to be approachable enough that you can make it easier for others to help your child. Make a conscious choice to stay open to people who want to come into your life or the life of your child and be supportive. Don't miss them because of what has happened in the past.

## YOU WILL SELDOM LIVE UP TO THE STANDARDS YOU SET FOR YOURSELF

This is true for most parents to some extent, but focusing on the gap between what you think you should be doing and what you are doing is deadly for parents who are raising kids with special needs. Sometimes your house is messier than you ever envisioned it would be. The laundry is piling up and you've eaten more take-out and frozen pizza lately than is healthy. None of your kids get enough one-on-one time.

It's also true that you're going to doctor's appointments, to therapy, and to your child's school more than most other parents can imagine. It's imperative to realize how ridiculous it is to think you can live up to the unrealistic standards you imagined. Find the humor in such an assumption and let it go. Your goal for today is to trust that you're doing the best you can and that the most important things are being taken care of.

## Learning to share information about your kiddo is a gift you give to yourself and to the world

You marvel at your kiddo's determination and how joyful they feel when they accomplish something new. Every single day you're touched by how they change your family. You're all learning about compassion and patience. You finally understand what unconditional love really looks like.

You really do want to talk about your kid and how proud you are of them, but you're often hesitant to do so. You're afraid your friends will feel sorry for you instead of being happy for your steps forward. You're afraid they won't know how to respond or that they might decide that being around you is too painful or uncomfortable.

Do it anyway. Believe that people who care about you really do want to know what's going on with your child, though they might not be sure it's okay to ask. Share information about your child and give your friends and family permission to ask questions. Do it even if it's a bit out of your comfort zone. It will make you much less isolated and can go a long way to opening new avenues for your child to build a larger support system.

## The financial reality of what it takes to care for your child can feel insurmountable

Most of your friends seem to think that there's some magic resource that helps you with medical expenses. They think insurance or even the government has your back. But for most of you the reality is far different. You might have to mortgage your house or take out loans. Sometimes you go without necessities. You're often afraid about your finances.

Let go of shame you feel about your money situation. Shame implies that you're not worthy; that you have somehow been irresponsible. The deadliest thing about shame is that it causes you to isolate yourself and to keep secrets from people you care about. Isolating yourself is a luxury you cannot afford. Don't give your financial situation the power to keep you isolated from your support system.

## Progress for your kiddo is joyful and you're grateful for even the smallest steps forward

You relish those moments when something happens that you didn't expect. You particularly cherish the days when your child has been working toward a goal and masters it. However, if you make your happiness dependent on their progress, neither one of you will ever win. They'll watch your reactions and feel like a failure when you're not happy.

A healthy balance between acceptance of what is and gratitude for achievements is tough to achieve. There's no way to get it right all the time. There will be times when progress seems nonexistent. There might even be times when your child isn't interested in trying very hard. Sometimes you'll need to back off and trust their process.

## You find yourself sad over things you thought you were over long ago

It can happen at the strangest times. Around graduation time you can be walking past the graduation cards or party decorations and have tears running down your cheeks. When your kid ages out of the system, you may not know what's going to happen for them. You might pass a group of teens laughing together at the mall and feel like you've been kicked in the gut because your kid may never have friends to laugh with. Will they have something to look forward to after high school? Will they be able to work?

Why are you thinking about this today? Today is a good day and there's no reason to be worrying! You were perfectly happy ten minutes ago! Unexpected emotions just come with the territory. It doesn't mean you're not willing to accept your kid. It doesn't mean your progress toward finding peace isn't real. It doesn't mean anything. It just is what it is. What's important is to just let it be. Don't try to fix it, and don't feel ashamed. Let it pass through you and settle where it needs to.

## One of the most important things you've become is an advocate for your child

Your child needs you to speak for them. You know them best so you can usually do it better than anybody else. Your biggest challenge is to advocate with an open mind and face each new situation with a clean slate.

You want to be able to put aside the disappointments of the past. With every new teacher or therapist or social worker, start from the assumption that their intention is to be the most helpful they can be. Make a conscious choice not to start out from a defensive stance. If you let go of defensiveness, professionals on your team find it much easier and more pleasant to work with you. If you keep an open mind and are willing to listen without judgment, your child always gets better care.

## Sometimes people look past your child like they're not even there

You can't always tell if they really don't notice or if they notice and are so uncomfortable with your child's differences that they don't want to see. Either way, your reactions vary depending on your mood. Sometimes you can feel your face get hot with rage. Sometimes your heart breaks and you want to burst into tears. Sometimes you're having a good enough day to have no feelings at all.

Whatever your response might be, it's fine. You may not be able to choose how you feel. What you can do is feel the feelings and not be afraid of them. Register them, then let them go. Your feelings really have nothing to do with the people around you. They're yours. The faster you acknowledge them, the faster their power to ruin your day is diminished. This is the best way to not allow others' reactions to your child to affect the quality of your day.

## Some days it feels like you can't do this for one more day

You feel like you're walking in quicksand. The harder you fight, the more you sink. Your temper is short, or you have no reaction at all. It seems like you'll never be hopeful again. You cannot escape this kid. You cannot fight with one more teacher or insurance company. You cannot get ready for one more IEP meeting. You just *can't*.

Despite your best efforts, or how well you take care of yourself, these days will come. You need to be ready. Do you have a plan for them?

Knowing that these hopeless days happen makes it worth it to put in the work it takes to build a support system. Find a way to help each other through those days. Other parents might take your kid when you need them to, and you take theirs when they need you to. Or it might be a family member or a spouse. If there's no one you can turn to, consider establishing a respite fund – money you tuck away to hire support when you're running on empty.

If none of the options that involve others are open to you, figure out a way to give yourself a bit of a break.

Put your kiddo in a safe place and take a shower or sit outside. Leave the dishes or skip something that can wait. It doesn't matter how simple or elaborate your plans are for hopeless days – you just need to have one.

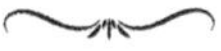

# CHAPTER 5

# Advice

After I rode a three-wheeled bike in the first Minnesota Red Ribbon Ride (a fundraiser benefiting agencies that provide services for people with HIV/AIDS) in 2002, I opened a business selling bikes to special kids and their families. I rode in that event to honor some friends I had lost to AIDS, but I accidently discovered how much cycling could enrich my life. I got off the bike and announced that we needed a bike shop for special needs families.

I started my bike business thinking that my primary customers were the kiddos. What I discovered in those years was that my deepest connections were with parents. That's when I learned how amazing you all are. Until that time I had never considered that my CP gave me a story that people might need to hear. Watching and loving special families was a whole new world. I had spent all my adult life trying to prove I wasn't different. I never wanted a place in the special needs community. It was loving you that showed me that *all* of me was a gift, even the parts of me I had spent a lifetime trying to hide.

During those years parents asked me how they could best help their children. In this chapter I'm happy to share some of the things that seemed to help. I hope they help you find some direction if you need it.

## Encourage your child to push themselves past their comfort zone

Teach them to believe they can accomplish things that seem impossible. With effort, self-confidence, and hard work, they can do anything they put their minds to.

Wanting to do this consistently, and doing it, are two very different things. If you see your child struggling and getting frustrated, your inclination is to jump in and help. You want them to feel safe and loved. But if you're not careful you'll make them feel helpless. Finding a balance between the two is an ongoing challenge, yet the greatest gift you can give your child is independence. Be willing to do what's hard for them today so their future can be brighter.

## On the joyful days, let the joy of the moment just be

There are days with your kiddo that are unbelievably magical – days when you're overwhelmed by how grateful you are that they're here, and it feels like a time to celebrate. These days can come when nothing much is happening or changing, but can also show up during periods of struggle. The important thing is to savor them whenever they happen. Don't overthink it. Just let it be.

## TODAY, FOCUS ON HAVING FAITH IN YOUR CHILD

Even on the toughest days your child is determined to survive and thrive.

You spend more hours than you care to admit feeling guilty. You wonder if you were careless. You wonder if God is angry with you. Was something in you so broken that your child must pay the price for it? The games your mind and heart can play are insidious.

Today, honor your special kid in a new way. Assume that this life is the perfect one for them. You've seen how they touch hearts and change lives. Even if you can only believe it for one minute, start there. Be a coach, a manager, and a champion for this special, perfect life. Things are as they should be.

## Become a champion of Plan B

Before you had your kiddo, you could be reasonably sure of how things were going to go. Trips could be planned for and looked forward to. You could make commitments to your friends and they could count on you without fail.

Life with a special child means everything on your calendar is written in pencil. Sometimes even the best set of plans falls through. Any effort can become a life-changing cause for celebration or a touch-and-go situation that comes out of nowhere. That's just the way it is.

Let go of guilt when plans change. You're showing up to do the next right thing. Celebrate that and give yourself permission to go with whatever needs to be done in any given moment.

## Acceptance is the gold standard of what you should strive to achieve when you're raising a child with a disability

It can be a lot like chasing the Holy Grail. It's easy to believe that acceptance is some magic place you will get to one day and all your problems will be over, but when you're having a tough time you blame yourself for not having enough of this thing called acceptance.

I don't think that's how acceptance works. Rather, it comes to you moment by moment. Acceptance is peace that comes when you're living in the present moment. When you're right here. When you simply feel the feelings you feel right now. When you can see the situation you're in just for what it is right now. It's a gift, and it comes to you the more you're willing to let yourself be. Right here, right now.

You don't arrive at acceptance and live there forever, so don't punish yourself when you don't feel it. It will come to you when you're loving yourself the most, one minute at a time.

## Letting go of a specific outcome is not the same as giving up

Even if you do everything right and you're the world's absolute best parent, sometimes the results you want are not going to happen. You might even have to face the fact that what you're sure you cannot survive is exactly what's happening.

But you're so much stronger than you think. Feeling like you're going to crumble into a million little pieces is not the same thing as actually crumbling, because even on the worst days, there is tomorrow. You don't even need to believe you will survive. Just breathe and the next step forward will come.

Letting go of an idea always makes way for a new way of thinking. Surrendering to what *is* comes from great strength. Trust yourself on the darkest days.

## It's okay to laugh

Having a child with a disability takes up most of the space in your brain. The future can feel like a black hole that you have no control over. Laughing at anything about your life seems unthinkable. This darkness will lift. I promise.

Like most things in your life, what you laugh at will probably change. I watched a group of mothers with special kiddos get on the trolley at the zoo. One had an oxygen tank, they all had wheelchairs, and two of the kids were blind. I was sitting close enough to hear them talking about how funny they must look to folks watching them, and they were laughing – laughing hard, like any group of good friends out for a day with the kiddos. They were comfortable and easy with each other. They found joy in the ridiculousness of everyday things. And they laughed. That might have been the day I decided I needed to write this book.

You will laugh too. Your new normal will be normal, and there will be joy in it. I promise.

## Don't assume that your child feels as you do

Watching your child struggle can be unbearable. You watch them with so much love, put yourself in their place, and imagine they feel as you would. But their experience is not yours.

Your child has their own feelings about their disability, and they'll find a way to deal with it in their own time. Some days will be tough, for sure. Some will be glorious and your child will be on the top of the world. They'll come to cherish some parts of their special life and will be a little sad about others. But that's theirs to do. You can get stuck assuming things that aren't true, but it's much worse in your mind than it is for them. If you get pulled down into feeling sorry for them you won't be able to help them, so have faith in their process.

## Be patient with yourself – life changes in a spiral

One of the hardest things about this life is that feelings you thought you dealt with keep coming back. You've worked hard on not letting your anger about having a special kid overtake your feelings about your life, and then all of a sudden something happens and you're right back there, angry and rageful; and you really thought that part was over. This happens and it seems hopeless. You think, "Why can't I do this better? Why can't I be better than this and keep it together?"

The answer is that when you dealt with those feelings the last time you were in a different place. Not worse. Not better. Just different. You're just experiencing them again with a new set of tools – things you've learned since last time. This is part of the living, growing, loving cycle. When old feelings show up, it means you're present. You're showing up in your life – willing to live it, willing to feel it, and willing to keep moving. You really are a hero!

## Being with typical families can be lonely

Spending time with parents who have typical kids can feel quite lonely. It can feel awkward to talk about your milestones with excitement when they seem so inconsequential compared to what your friends' kids are doing. You often keep your mouth shut because you don't want folks to think they need to feel sorry for you or your kiddo.

This kind of isolation can be deadly. It can feed on your feelings of shame and guilt. Hiding your life might seem easier and more considerate. You may choose this path from time to time, but silence doesn't mean you belong. These may be people you know but they're not your tribe.

Make an effort to find other families that are walking this journey. You need them and they need you. It might be the last thing you want to do – it might go entirely against your nature and far outside your comfort zone. Do it anyway. If you don't find a good match right away, keep trying. It's worth it. Trust me on this!

## People who work in large systems are sometimes as frustrated as you are

School systems can be hard. They can be infuriating. Most of the people who make the rules that affect your life and the life of your child in major ways have no idea what your life is like. They have no idea what your kid needs on a given day. They're trying to stretch too few dollars way further than really makes sense. Despite all this, you will amaze yourself over and over by how hard you're willing to fight for your kiddo.

The trickiest part of this can be separating the problem with the system from the caregivers who are working with your child. They may be just as frustrated as you are. It's much easier for them to help you and your child if you don't take your frustrations out on them just because they're there.

When a system I must deal with treats me unfairly because of my disability, my first instinct can be to want to attack everybody. I've learned the hard way that this isn't the most effective way to get what I need. If I cut folks a little slack and assume they're not the enemy, it's amazing what can happen.

There will always be times when pushing hard and making people uncomfortable is the only option. I can do that and so can you. But gentleness and a little trust are usually the best option.

## What seems like a mistake can often be what is needed to get to the next best solution

You make so many decisions for your special kiddo. Some of them are life-altering with huge consequences. To say that the pressure to get it right every time can be overwhelming is certainly an understatement.

The good news is that you're an expert on what's good for your child. You know them better than anybody. Your gut is tuned in to them in amazing ways. Nobody is better equipped to speak for them than you. Even when you don't feel like that's true, it is.

You read and study all the most current research. Armed with the facts and the support of a good team of professionals, your killer instincts are amazing. Most of the time you can be sure that your decisions are the right ones.

Then there are the other times – times when the outcome of a decision is not at all what you expected or hoped for. When a decision you made turns out to have negative consequences for your child, it's devastating. It can stop you dead in your tracks and make you question everything.

On the rare occasion that you regret a choice you made, you still need to trust it. Even a decision that doesn't turn out as you planned moves you closer to the next right decision.

Your child needs you to be confident. They trust you every day. You cannot know where the decisions of today will lead you tomorrow. What counts is today. What counts is putting one foot in front of the other and moving forward. There's no other way to get to the next best thing.

## You're not in denial when you're hopeful

One of the first things parents always want to know after a diagnosis is what they can expect. "Will our child be able to walk?" "What about talking or reading?" "Will they have developmental delay?" Some doctors are agonizingly vague. Some really try to give you the best information they have. At best it's an educated guess.

Doctors told my mother I might have some cognitive delay. (This was the early fifties so I'm sure the R word was involved.) My mom just kept saying, "Well maybe, but I don't think so," in a very thick southern drawl.

My best advice is to use what you're told as a guideline. It's a piece of information along with so many you will be given, and nobody knows for sure what will happen. Just because you hope for more or something different doesn't mean you're in denial. It means you want to help your child achieve the best life possible.

Don't be invested in any certain outcome. Buckle up for this ride and enjoy it. Bring "the best you got" on any given day, whatever that is. Trust that your kiddo will do the same. The outcome will unfold in its own time. Love always wins.

## Don't be a roadblock. Sometimes the best thing you can do is shut up and watch

It's your job to protect your child from a world that's not built for them and save them from people who want to make them so much less than they are. Yet there are days when you're ready to take on the world in a not-so-good way. Sometimes you'll need to speak up, maybe make some people uncomfortable.

But what your kid often needs most is for you to be quiet and let them find their own way. Let them try even if what they want more than anything seems impossible. Help them understand that trying is what matters, and success is a bonus. A determined effort is what they need to learn to trust and value. That much they have control over. The outcome? Maybe, maybe not.

If we're confident enough to try to find a way to go after what we want, regardless of disability, we're always free. When we're afraid to try or afraid to fail, then disability really does win.

So hang on for this one. It's a delicate balance. I guarantee you'll screw this up more than once. That's okay. Try anyway. Some days you will hit it just right. Trust yourself. Trust your kid. If you stay out of the way, amazing things can happen!

## Remember to honor that person you were in the first days. You're no longer that person, but that person will show up in your life now and again. Welcome them!

Your child and the journey you're taking together change you forever in ways that will surprise you for the rest of your life. You will defend your child fiercely and take on entire institutions to get them what they need. You will learn to embrace being the squeaky wheel and won't care much when you realize you have become *that* parent. You will be able to face the world with unwavering hope when people around you tell you there's not much reason for it. You will do these things because of what you see in those beautiful eyes. You will do them because of the secret communications you have with your child when nobody else is around, because in those moments you can see the beauty of the remarkable person who is your child. Relish the warrior that you're becoming. Be proud. Be confident. Be sure.

There's a part of you that's still the shell-shocked parent from the first days. The person you were then, feeling like you were walking around with no skin on, is still a part of you. Embrace that parent from the first days. They will show up every now and then. Don't panic. It doesn't mean the warrior in you isn't real. The warrior is real and returns without fail. When you think you're folding, be gentle with yourself. When you're afraid, be afraid. Let those moments pass through you. Trust that what you've learned and the growth you've worked so hard for are always there. Whatever you're feeling in this very moment is just fine.

## It is OK to plan activities with your typical children only

Your special kiddo doesn't have to participate in every activity your family experiences. If you have typical children, there's a constant battle between being fair to your special kiddo and allowing your typical children to have the childhood and experiences they deserve. If your other kiddos want to go on an adventure with you that would be impossible for their sibling to participate in, give yourself permission to do that. Leave your special one in the hands of somebody you trust and go for it. Enjoy the freedom of feeling like everybody else for an afternoon, a day, or the duration of a trip.

## What makes your child special has nothing to do with their disability

You and those around you might refer to yourself as a "special needs parent" and your child as a "special needs child." It's true that these labels are sometimes useful. They help you identify your tribe – the people whose lives are like yours in so many ways. They give you a convenient shorthand with which to communicate some of the realities you're living.

When I look back on my growing-up years, one of the things I remember most about my mom is that she often reminded me that there were some special things about me. I was funny, she said. I was kind. I was smart. I worked hard. But never once did she say, "What is most special about you is that you have a disability." It never occurred to me that CP was what made me most special. Even when dealing with it seemed to take up so much of my energy, I always felt that there were other things about me that were much more important.

I promise you that your kid will learn from you how little of their life is defined by their disability.

## Sometimes tough love means allowing your kid to be uncomfortable

I hate the phrase "tough love." I hate to think about somebody "tough loving" me. I hate those words when I'm trying to decide if what I'm doing is something I should be doing *for* or *to* somebody else for their own good. Tough love is something we talk about and often try to do, but it's always murky. Nobody gets it right all the time. The payoff comes later, so you might see it but you might not.

But tough love is vitally important for your kiddo. Helplessness is deadly for everybody, but particularly so for kids learning to be in the world with a disability. So, yes, you do need to allow your kiddo to struggle when they need to in order to figure out that they can find a way to do many things for themselves.

It's important to help those we love not be afraid of struggling and doing the hard work, even when it seems like the desired outcome isn't possible. The more your child is willing to keep working when they want to give up, the more freedom they will have in the long run.

## If you're going to accept what your true feelings are, you must be willing to accept the feelings of others

So much of the journey with your kiddo is about accepting your feelings about living with a disability you did not plan on. I still believe that my own feelings are the scariest thing about being human. My guess is that sometimes this is true for you too. I also believe that the greatest joy of my life is learning to relax and let my feelings be whatever they are.

There is another side to that same coin. If you're going to allow yourself the freedom to be and feel whatever is true, give the same freedom to other people in your life, no matter how frightening that might be. Let the people who love your child have their own grief and their own process for finding acceptance.

## DON'T HOLD ON TO BELIEFS THAT NO LONGER SERVE YOU

Your most basic beliefs about how things work can keep you stuck. But if you believe that the world isn't fair, you won't find lasting peace. If you believe that good things happen to you because you earned them by being a good person, you can never forgive yourself for whatever horrible thing you did that caused your kid to have a disability. Every reason you come up with to explain it falls flat when you think it through. So the only answer that works is that you did not cause your child's differences and neither did they. Period.

## Today, remember to be more playful

Laughing at some of the silly things you do puts things in perspective in a way that nothing else does. Raising a special child can make that harder. You spend so much time questioning your decisions and struggling with feelings that don't make any sense that you can forget to just enjoy how delightful laughter can be. Trust that making time to be playful is always worth it.

## Spend time being grateful for the gifts you've received from your special child

We've all heard people say, "My child has taught me more than I've ever been able to teach her." It sounds like a cliché until you begin to identify those things in your own life: patience, compassion, and the power of unconditional love.

You can see changes in yourself from loving a child with special needs. When you begin to identify them and name them, you can be grateful for them.

The mysteries of why some children are born with differences or catastrophic disabilities are far beyond what you can understand in this lifetime. I do not for one minute believe that the Universe intended to sacrifice the happiness of a child to further your growth. Even so, it's good to acknowledge the gifts that have come to you because of the child you have.

## Chasing Normal is a lose lose proposition

This kind of obsession is deadly. If you stay there, your spirit dies a little bit every day. Your child might pick up from you that you're not okay with who they are.

There's a difference between a frantic search for one magic answer that will bring you to "normal" and an educated search for information and research that might be helpful. Focus on the latter while accepting what is.

## Take time to give yourself credit for what you do

With all the muck and the crazy feelings, do you know that you're doing okay? Some days are clearly better than others. What people think you do and what you actually do are sometimes vastly different. But in your truest heart, where nobody really sees, do you truly understand that you're doing okay?

Work at knowing that your best on any given day is enough. You are enough, and you're absolutely the best person to take care of your special child.

## The things you're likely to worry about most have not yet happened

You can work yourself into a frenzy over what your child's future will look like. You can lose sleep any night over the horror pictures you conjure up in your mind.

It's true that there aren't enough services for special needs kids as they transition into adulthood. Even so, endless worry is not helpful. Commit to developing a plan. Seek out families and programs that seem to be having the most success. Stay open to learning about good options. Trust your problem-solving skills. Over time you've gotten better and better at making decisions and finding what you need. Your skills will continue to grow. When you need to know, you'll know.

## Take care of yourself well, both physically and mentally

There are certainly physical components of self-care that you must address, but your kid is also counting on you to find your spiritual path.

When you first knew that your child was going to be different than expected and you began to see how hard their life was going to be, any faith you had might have gone out the window. Your understanding of God and what you could count on might have collapsed in a big hurry. The way you thought the world was supposed to work if you were a good person was no longer true.

You don't need to have all the answers. You don't need to pretend that any of this makes sense. Living in the present moment is your quickest road to a peaceful heart. Pay attention to when you make good choices and give yourself credit when you feel your confidence growing. These tiny steps are enough. Little by little you will have faith again. You will have what you need to find peace with your new normal.

## Pay attention and spot the ways your child touches the lives of the people around them

Your child will touch others in the same way he touches your heart. You know this is true because you can see people's faces soften when they talk to him. Your child teaches the people around him compassion and patience. The determination and fighting spirit you see in your child inspires others too.

This is the work your child came to do. He is a gift to the world. It is part of your job to share him with others. People need the gifts your child has to offer them.

## CHAPTER 6

# Love Letters

The entries in this chapter are written as tiny love letters to your special child, to you, and to the people who love and support your family. These are all thoughts about love that I have over and over. Some are based on lessons I learned from my mother. Some are based on things I wish we had talked about but didn't.

I hope they bring you joy and a smile or two. I hope some of them give you a new way to think about how you want to relate to the special child you love.

## My precious, beautiful child, I love you

I'm proud that you're mine. I want you to know that you're such a great gift to me and to the world. All of us are better because you're here. I'll never understand why you were born with what appear to be limits, but I see in your eyes that you have a special connection to the Universe. You move more slowly and don't miss a thing. You stay in the present moment in a way that I'll always envy. Be proud of who you are and who you're helping all of us to become.

I spend a lot of my time helping you do day-to-day things. There are rhythms to our days and nights that tie us together. Some days both of us hate it, but most days it feels like a private dance that nobody else knows the steps to. There's joy in it that I never expected.

## Do you know that you're the most amazing person I know?

I see how hard you work at being better. I see the days that are impossibly hard. I see the times you're so proud when you learn something new. I *love* those days.

Just in case we get so busy that I forget to say it often enough – I adore you!

## Today I can speak up for you when you cannot

Because I know you best and am lucky enough to be your person, I sometimes know exactly what to say. Loving you so fiercely has given me courage and confidence that I didn't have before. Until you, I had no idea how much of a warrior I could truly be.

I often wonder if you have any idea how you affect the people around you. I watch how people are when they talk to you. It makes them softer. It makes them gentler. They slow down and pay attention. That's one of the great gifts you bring to the world. Sometimes I think that must be part of your purpose. I wish I were better at finding words to let you know how special that is.

## SOME DAYS I'M AWFUL AT EVERYTHING

I'm grumpy and out of sorts. Too tired, too worried, too stressed. You, more than anybody else, are just as glad to see me on those days as on any other day. First thing in the morning, even at your sleepiest, you have a smile for me. You give me that look that says you know I will show up to do our day no matter what. I love that about you.

## Here's what I promise

I will do the best I can today to plan for your future – maybe do some research about options if that makes sense. But then I will let it go. The best thing I can do today for your future is to be as present for you as I can and help you focus on what you're learning today.

## Sometimes simply watching you makes me smile down to my toes

We can play together and make each other laugh. Nothing that I must do today is so important that I cannot take a bit of time to play. You're much better at this than I am, so you'll need to be patient with me. Thank you for reminding me to take the time to play.

I keep saying to you, "I just want you to be happy."

If you see me happy and committed to my own happiness, the chances that you will grow up happy are much greater. I want to take more time to enjoy how happy it makes me to be with you.

## Let me make this very clear: I love you

I will always love you, no matter what. I don't want you to question that, ever. I know our life is not typical. I know I need to help you in ways that most parents don't help their children. I know there are some great things about being a parent that might not happen as I parent you. I know you know that too, or you will someday, and it doesn't matter; even if I'm tired or frustrated, it doesn't matter. You are and always will be one of the greatest gifts of my life.

I know there are days when you struggle with the effects of your disability. Sometimes you're open about it and sometimes you keep it to yourself. I want you to know how much I respect the way you deal with it, even on your toughest days. Remember, my dear, you don't have to hide your feelings about it, whatever they are. Even when it feels like your limits will do you in, I know they won't. I'll bet on you any day.

## I HAVE A NOTE TODAY FOR MY TYPICAL CHILDREN

I love you. Your hearts are so big, and you seem to know what to do for your sibling who often needs extra help. More than any of us, you see the kid first, and the disability doesn't seem to matter much. I know that sometimes what you need must wait. I know that you would rather be at a playground than in a therapy waiting room. I know that I never seem to be able to make any of it up to you, even when I intend to. Please know that I see you. I see what you do for this family. I see your kindness. I'm so proud of you.

## Thank you, my precious child

I love you in a way I didn't know existed. I'm becoming a far better person because of you. You've helped set me on a spiritual journey that I could not have imagined before you were here. Somehow, in the cosmos, in a way that I do not begin to understand, you and I were melded together to do this magical dance. There's a bond between us that's very rare. Few experience it, and fewer still understand how wonderful it is. I think we somehow chose each other, and I would choose you again, a million times.

## Do you know that I love you just because I do?

So does everybody else who loves you. Your job growing up is not to try to make people love you; it's to become the kind of person who doesn't put up roadblocks to people who have decided they want to love you. This is one of life's great lessons, and I've spent a lifetime trying to remember it. My guess is that you will do that too. I think it's part of the human condition.

Never think you need to compromise what you believe to make people like you.

## Some days I spend time wondering why you have your disability

Is it my fault? Did I do something to make it happen? Was I careless? If it is my fault, can you forgive me? Sometimes I frantically look over research to prove to myself it's not my fault, or to prove that it is so I can justify how guilty I feel. This is the crazy stuff that goes on in my head, and I really do know it's pointless and wastes my energy. Even so, I do it anyway.

I'm sure you have some version of this that you do in your own head: "Is my disability my fault?" "My parents' fault?" The truth is I have no idea why. Neither do you. I believe that someday we'll know. But more than anything I believe that right this minute you and I are both doing exactly what we're supposed to be doing. We both bring unique and wonderful gifts to the world because of the life we're leading.

## THERE AREN'T MANY THINGS I'M SURE ABOUT, BUT ONE IS THAT HAPPINESS DEPENDS ON A GRATEFUL HEART

In any situation we have much to appreciate. It's not the circumstances we find ourselves in that make us grateful, it's the ability to see that we're blessed and to recognize the great gifts we've been given. I hope I'm living in such a way that you recognize this in me. If I can help you live in gratitude, it's one of the greatest gifts I can give you.

## When people look at you and see only your disability, I hope you remember that's not who you are

I wonder whether you can look at people who don't have disabilities and see that they have struggles too. I hope so.

At times it does seem like your disability is all we ever have time to think about, and that if you didn't have it everything in the world would be perfect. This is not true. All people have pain, disappointments, fears, and suffering at some time or another. That's what draws us together. I want you to understand that you're more like everybody else than you know.

"Dance like nobody's watching" is a quote that comes to my mind often. I want that phrase to be a key to how you live your life. For most things that you really want to do, you'll be able to find a way. It might take a ridiculous amount of time, but the adventure of finding *your* way can be priceless.

The secret is this: When you think you look silly or stupid trying to find a way to learn something new, what others actually see is what a miracle you are

– how brave you are and how much ingenuity you have. What you actually do is make others more willing to try things themselves. So go for it! Dance, and know that you're making the world beautiful.

## I want you to be able to tell that I love you by how I treat you

I want you to be able to see it and feel it even on the hardest days. If you accidently make a mess, I want to remember to clean it up quietly so you'll know that I understand that accidents happen. I want you to be relaxed when you're with me because you're confident I won't blow up if something goes wrong.

Sometimes I'm snappier than I intend to be. Sometimes I lose my temper over stupid stuff. When this happens, know that I'm only human; it's never ever about you.

## For my friends

The ones who have stayed. When a special child is born, it can be hard on friendships. My life is hard to understand. I know that you cannot always count on me to follow through on plans we make. But what I want you to know is that it's always a disappointment to me when I cancel. That we have plans in the first place is a lifeline.

There must be a lot of times when you struggle to figure out what to say about my kiddo. You wonder how much to ask about. Sometimes I struggle with how much to share. We often get it right and the sharing between us feels magic. I know you hear me, I know you love me, and I know you'll be present on the toughest days.

Sometimes we struggle to get the balance right, and things feel a bit awkward. For me it's always worth it to try again. I love you to the moon and back.

## For the writers

I love that people before me have written about special needs kiddos and the journeys parents are on as they raise them. I love that people who come after me will do the same. This is sacred work. Reading about families like mine has often allowed me to take another step; to make the next decision. Words from parents and people living with and loving people with disabilities let me know I'm not alone. They let me know I'm not crazy. They give me courage to share my own story.

## This is a love letter to me, reminding me that my gifts to the world are uniquely mine and that I'm responsible for making the best possible use of my talents

If I discount my gifts and assume nobody needs what I have to offer, the world misses out. Intellectually I know this is true, but I struggle to always believe it in my heart. So, to my beautiful self, I send this reminder.

Nobody in the world knows exactly what I know in the way that I know it. There are people around me who need my unique gifts. It might be my art, or my words. It might be an idea, a way to make things better. It might be the patient, quiet way I listen. No matter what my gifts are, the world needs me to share them.

## For the doctors who work with my kiddo

I love that you decided to dedicate your work life to kids like mine. I know there are certainly easier ways to make a living. I appreciate all the hours you spent studying to get there and the money you must have spent for the training you needed. We envision that you have more money than you could ever spend, your children and marriages are perfect, and you know everything. I bet most of that's not true and that your lives are more like ours than we imagine. So thank you. Thank you for the sleepless nights, and thank you for the hours you spend away from your own children so you can take care of mine.

## To my child's teacher

You hold a special place in my heart. You probably spend more time with my child than any other person besides me. They have a relationship with you that they don't have with anybody else. You introduce them to the world in ways they understand. You get to see their face when they learn something new for the very first time. I love you because you seem to know when to push them a little further than they think they can go. I love you for loving them and valuing them.

## This love note is for the person I was when I first began to realize that my child had some needs I was not expecting

In those days I was so lost, so scared. I thought I would cry every day for the rest of my life. I was sure there was no way I could ever give my child what they needed and that I would never be able to provide the joyful life I wanted for them.

I wish I could go back and tell that person that things will be okay. I wish I could let them know that they will grow stronger; that there is an army of supportive parents and families that they don't know about yet. And the best surprise of all is that this little person will turn out to be their biggest hero.

## It sometimes amazes me how rare and precious we really are

I have no idea why you and I were chosen for this life. If we look at the statistics, the chance of having a disability is low. Most studies say about 5 percent of the population is born with a disability; so we're a rare pair.

Yet the world needs us. We teach people about love and patience in a very specific way. We make each other better. It's rare and beautiful indeed.

## CHAPTER 7

# What I Know Now

The seven-year-old me who cried because she couldn't skate turned out just fine. My mother and I survived my shaving my eyebrow because I was angry that I couldn't walk better. In fact, the eyebrow thing became one of our funniest family stories.

I still cherish the Holiday on Ice trips and the Christmas parade when the Brownies rode in the Candyland truck. I remember that my mom and dad threw the jump rope for hours so I could learn to do it well enough to jump rope at school.

Your kids, too, will have memories of precious times when you made them feel special and raised them in ways that felt perfect. They will also have memories of when it was so painful to be different that they weren't sure they could ever survive it. No matter how much you love them, or how creative you are, they will have these moments. It comes with the territory.

There are some great gifts that come with being different too. When you're used to being last at most things you try, you know you might look silly when you decide you want to learn something new. I love swimming and snorkeling, but always wanted to learn to scuba dive. So at sixty, guess what I did. I learned.

Before the first class I thought about calling to let them know that I had CP and might need some extra support. I decided against it, and just showed up and acted like I didn't notice. It was kind of funny really. On my first attempt I ended up turtled at the bottom of the pool, unable to move because the tanks were too heavy. I started to panic; then I remembered that I could breathe. I figured that eventually somebody would retrieve me. They did.

I think they kept thinking I would eventually quit, but I was having a blast. I made it through the classroom/pool portion of certification, then went to the Dutch Antilles for my open water certification. I've been to the Great Barrier Reef and I dived the cenotes in Mexico. –"I've seen a real Mayan pot, deep in an underwater cave."

I have ridden a bike over two hundred and fifty miles in three and a half days. I've done stand-up comedy. I'm a reasonably good cook and a better-than-average poker player. If I could snap my fingers and be a great dancer or an amazing athlete, I would choose that, but not for one minute would I be willing to give up the me I've turned out to be.

I know now that I'll be okay – more than okay – and so will your kiddos. We're far tougher than you think. Different is hard. Different has also made my life rich and profoundly joyful.

What I'm most sure of is that you'll be okay – more than okay. Trust that the people you need will show up. The answers you need will be found. Your amazing children will become their amazing selves. You will give them memories they will always cherish, and they will rise far beyond what you expect... I promise.

# About the Author

Sally Brown is a woman living with cerebral palsy.

She worked in the tech industry for twenty years. In 2003 she rode the first Minnesota Red Ribbon Ride on a three-wheeled bike to honor the memory of her friends lost to AIDS. Then she switched her focus to providing bikes to kids and adults with special needs. She founded Every Kid Mobility, an adaptive bike company she operated from 2004 to 2009. During that time she also created a line of crutches and mobility devices personalized with photos and art.

In 2006 her first novel, *The Big Red Bike*, was released. A second release of that book is coming soon. She speaks publicly about her life as a person thriving with a disability. Her focus has always been on parents raising special needs children.

Her favorite hobby is scuba diving, which she does not do nearly enough. She loves cycling and is obsessed with three-wheeled bikes.

Sally lives in San Diego with her wife, Vickie. They own a property that is home to their extended family. Sally describes herself as a professional grandmother to twelve- year-old twins, Ava and Dylan.

For a free printable poster of The 10 Things, visit SallyRossBrown.com

Acknowledgements

First acknowledgement goes to my amazing mother, Mary Leila Bradley Ross, who shares this story with me. The saying goes, "The apple doesn't fall far from the tree." In my case, I certainly hope that is true.

I also would like to thank my publisher, Lynne Klippel and her staff at Thomas Noble books. Without your love and endless encouragement, and an occasional kick in the pants, this book would have never happened. Your talent makes my work better. Your friendship makes my life better. I am forever grateful.

I would also like to thank the Shimmering Waters Writers' group. A little piece of each of you is in these pages. I am honored to be in your company. I am always in awe of your talent.

Dr Jill Gettings, thank you so much for your feedback on the early chapters of this book. Your invaluable feedback helped me shape this book into the story I wanted to share.

# Index

Made in the USA
Monee, IL
26 September 2020

42829562R10125